Open Past,
Open Future

Open Past, Open Future

my journey across the borders
of the mind and nations

S.P. Rawal

RUPA

Published by
Rupa Publications India Pvt. Ltd 2021
7/16, Ansari Road, Daryaganj
New Delhi 110002

Sales centres:
Allahabad Bengaluru Chennai
Hyderabad Jaipur Kathmandu
Kolkata Mumbai

Copyright © S.P. Rawal 2021
Photographs courtesy: S.P. Rawal

All rights reserved.
No part of this publication may be reproduced, transmitted,
or stored in a retrieval system, in any form or by any means,
electronic, mechanical, photocopying, recording or otherwise,
without the prior permission of the publisher.

The views and opinions expressed in this book are
the author's own and the facts are as reported by her
which have been verified to the extent possible,
and the publishers are not in any way liable for the same.

ISBN: 978-93-91256-98-2

Third impression 2021

10 9 8 7 6 5 4 3

The moral right of the author has been asserted.

Printed at Saurabh Printers Pvt. Ltd, Noida

This book is sold subject to the condition that it shall not, by way
of trade or otherwise, be lent, resold, hired out, or otherwise circulated,
without the publisher's prior consent, in any form of binding or cover
other than that in which it is published.

Dedication

I dedicate this humble effort, where I have looked into the past to prepare a collage of memories, to my revered parents; they were my visible and living Gods while they were around and, since then, a perpetual source of inspiration.

Dedication

Krishna, my beloved wife, understood and supported me through thick and thin till she breathed her last. Educating our children was always her priority, even when her own comfort and necessities had to be sacrificed.
Her abundant love for them and the values she imparted have formed the foundation of what they are today.
I will miss her until my last breath.

Her presence is felt even in her absence

*So far so good and let us hope for
the best in the future.*

CONTENTS

Foreword   xi

Introduction   xv

Part–I
The Past Beats Like A Second Heart

1. Early Years: Abundance   3
2. Partition: The Storm Within and Outside   6
3. Re-Starting from Zero   16
4. Joys of Childhood   20
5. Learnings from Kaithal   25
6. Moonlighting in College   34
7. Work and Marriage: A New Phase   40
8. The Joys of Family Life   52
9. A Tryst with Destiny!   57
10. My Children   88

11. A Dark Phase	91
12. My Diamonds, My Pearls, My Jewels and My Baghban	97
13. Rewiring not Retiring	105
Afterword	113
Acknowledgements	115
Messages	119

Part–II
Down Memory Lane: A Visual Journey

FOREWORD

SP, as I liked to call him, ends the introduction to this autobiography by saying, 'This is the story of an ordinary person.' But as you read the book, you will see how this is only his humility. He is, in fact, an extraordinary man. A man who has lived through some of the most fascinating times in modern history. His story is such that once you start reading it, you will not be able to put it down.

Although born into a wealthy and privileged family, SP soon experienced the horror of Partition: of having to flee his birthplace and manage from within in a refugee camp. From the start, however, he displayed his characteristic boundless energy, flair and resourcefulness. As a young boy, he helped his family—whether in the shop or the railway platform.

Two qualities shine throughout SP's incredible life: his love and devotion to his family and his commitment and enthusiasm for excelling at his work.

I first had the good fortune of meeting SP in 1994, when Gestetner appointed me as the Chief Executive of Gestetner India. On meeting him, I was immediately struck by his upright bearing, charisma, and ability to immediately engage with others. Initially, as a Senior General Manager, and then as a Vice President, he displayed excellent leadership skills. He led and motivated not only by virtue of his position but also through the love and respect he inspired among his fellow employees, customers and the community.

SP displayed an incredible commitment to Gestetner. He always strove to be the first and the best. Sometimes this involved tremendous personal sacrifices: being apart from his family, stationed in dangerous locations around the county. The company was fortunate to have him. It is also fortunate that his dedication and talent was recognized and harnessed. Throughout his career with Gestetner, SP displayed a steely determination and a strong desire to excel. He led from the front and his enthusiasm was contagious. He was always happy to share his knowledge with his staff and to celebrate their successes.

In this memoir, SP shows us how ambition and pride can coexist alongside a love for humanity and kindness. He shows how he triumphed over adversities and inspires us to do the same.

He also writes honestly about a number of things that he regards as having been mistakes he has made, and also shares with us his art of being able to learn from them. He shows us, in practical terms, how 'Life is 10% what happens to you and 90% how you react to it'

SP is rightly proud of the tremendous achievements of his children and grandchildren. But with characteristic humility, he gives all credit for this to his dear wife. His paternal qualities are, however, exceptional. Many employees at Gestetner loved and respected him in a way that was otherwise normally reserved only for fathers. This book is a wonderful record, not only for his immediate family and their descendants, but also for his Gestetner family and all humanity.

Paul Wilkinson
London

INTRODUCTION

Often, I have yearned to know something of my ancestors beyond the facts available in genealogical records. I imagined what trials, tribulations, joys, heartaches, sorrows, and achievements were traversed by those individuals from whom I descend. In the belief that my descendants may one day be consumed by a similar curiosity, I write this narrative of my life—a compilation of stories from my journal.

I approach this task with utmost humility. I have lived a life of deeds springing from the heart rather than the mind. I have endeavoured to make those around me happy and have always done what I believed God wanted me to do. I, however, also write this book with humility, keeping in mind that the decision to write an autobiography contains the assumption that what is set down in words should be worthy of preservation.

As such, I begin this narrative with a glimpse of my history, which begins with the background of my family—the Rawals. According to my grandparents, our heritage comes from Bappa Rawal. Bappa Rawal was a ruler in the Mewar region of present Rajasthan in India. Though it is difficult to accurately determine when exactly Bappa Rawal ruled, according to a 15th century text, *Ekalinga Mahatmya* or *Ekalinga Purana*, Bappa Rawal founded the Mewar Kingdom in 728 CE.

Over the centuries, many Mewari families migrated to nearby areas, primarily to regions in present-day Gujarat, which accounts for the strong presence of Rawals in the state today. A few other descendants opted to settle elsewhere; the family of my paternal great-grandparents, for example, settled in Punjab. To trace this scattered family history, I contacted our family pandit in Haridwar. Traditionally, when Hindu families visit Haridwar, whether on a pilgrimage or to perform the last rites and pray for the dearly departed, they record their names with a specific priest—a family pandit-Purohit, you may say—who keeps these records for generations.

The records with our Panditji go back seven generations, and most of the names sound Rajasthani. I have copies of these records, with signatures in a language called *landi*. I have seen my mother and grandmother wearing typical Rajasthani ghagras—a bright, swirling, pleated skirt that is long, embroidered and fitted with small round pieces of glass.

It is interesting to note that a neighbouring Marwari's influence (reputed to have in-born financial acumen) had affected my great grandparents who were in the finance business. My father too, started as a sahukar (a financier), but slowly shifted to being a zamindar.

What I gathered from my father was that his forefathers resided in a small village called Murdani, near Okara in present Pakistan. As they settled in the village, they started the business of money lending against mortgaging securities like silver-gold jewellery or land. In the process over the years, they accumulated big land holdings. They had done well by the standard of their time and had become enormously wealthy.

There was only one heir to this vast wealth—my grandfather, Hukam Chand Ji. My grandfather, in turn, had two children—a son (my father) and a daughter (my buaji). If I work backwards, the probable year of my father's birth would be around 1909. When he was 9 years, he lost his father.

My grandfather died young, falling to the influenza epidemic (Spanish Flu or Bombay Flu) of 1918-19, which claimed 14 million to17 million lives. People compare the present Covid-19 pandemic to that devastating epidemic, but medicine has, since, greatly advanced and I hope the vaccines will soon help life return to normal.

My father, from the age of nine, and his elder sister, from the age of twelve, were brought up by his grandfather, Ram Ditta Mal Shah and his younger brother, Channan Mal Shah. Unfortunately, after six or seven years, the elder brother also passed away, leaving the responsibility on the shoulders of the younger uncle grandfather (who also had his own children to look after). Their brotherly bonds were so strong that a brother would have thanklessly looked after the children of his brother with more love, care and affection than his own children. I have seen this trend with my own eyes. My own father-in-law took greater care of his brother's children more than his own. Children, too, would respect their uncles equally or more than their own parents. These were norms then. As an example, in those days, uncles were so respected that children would address their own father as 'uncle'. We too, till Partition, called our father, <u>Chacha ji</u> (uncle) and our mother,

Amma. It is only after Partition that we started calling them Pita ji and Mata ji.

My father, sometimes, would relate that his grandfather Channan Mal Shah, was looking after them (my father and his sister). As he was getting older and increasingly infirm, he decided that both the grandchildren should be married soon, and their property be divided between them.

My aunt, who was the older sibling, wed first. My father got married at the age of sixteen or seventeen to my mother, who was a few years younger than him at the time. Though they were wedded at a young age, this was deemed circumstantially necessary. I, too, was married at twenty-one, and my wife was barely seventeen. But times have changed. It is impossible to imagine children getting married at such an early age these days. In the case of my own children, they married close to their thirties, only after graduating from their desired field. This is the norm now. I have witnessed this transition and am part of a changing generation of parents.

In those days, gold was the ***most*** precious possession. The quantity of gold brought by the bride as dowry was the parameter for evaluating the social status of the family. I am told that at the time of her marriage, my mother was adorned with so many gold ornaments that even her legs, up to her knees, were covered with gold kangans.

After the wedding, Grandfather decided to divide the family wealth, which was in the form of silver coins. In those days, no formal banking system existed, and coins were stored in earthen pots, placed underneath the floors or within the walls of the mud houses.

When Grandfather was dividing the wealth between the

brother and the sister, it was not possible to count the coins. Instead, under the cover of night, they simply heaped iron vessels to the brim with the coins, alternately (and equally) handing over one vessel to the brother and another to the sister. The societal convention of giving the entire share to the son was not the norm in our family.

My father was a visionary right from his childhood, and was not keen to settle within the village. He wanted to shift to a region with more commerce. He decided to shift to Okara, a moderately metropolitan area with the biggest grain market in the region.

Thus, in the mornings, my parents would set off for Okara on a horse loaded with saddle bags, or kathi. The bags were filled with the silver coins and camouflaged with horse fodder. My parents rode off, together, on the same horse. This process continued for several days.

Arriving in Okara, my father bought a house and, in order to establish himself, he made it known in the city that he was willing to buy any house on sale. He also acted as a sahukar (financier), lending money on interest, with the borrower's house being mortgaged to him as security. I am told he owned almost half of the city soon. This was unknown to us, and we heard it in a classroom. Those days, students would sit in the class on the ground, in rows, on a jute rug, using a takhti (wooden board) for writing. Once, while I was writing, my ink got over and I was struggling, the Maulvi (teacher) sarcastically remarked that my father owned half of the city and I didn't have enough ink. This is when I found out about my father's wealth.

In one case, the borrower found himself unable to return

the money, and approached my father, begging not only for a waiver of interest but also for a reduction in the principal amount. My mother witnessed this scene where the borrower fell at my father's feet, begging and crying. She was so touched by this that she called my father inside, and asked him to stop mortgaging houses. She was a god-fearing woman, and had begun to believe that it was the ill-will of borrowers that had caused her three miscarriages. My mother believed that waiving the loan would generate goodwill, which could help her bear a child. Thus, my father not only wrote off the debt of this borrower, but also agreed to stop his mortgaging business.

Subsequently, my father diverted all his money to buying land. He continued lending money for business ventures. Before the Partition, he had extensive land holdings in four villages, especially in Tibbi on the bank of a tributary of river Ravi. Many farmers and labourers were employed in his fields. I remember visiting the fields with him once, when I was seven years old. I rode up on a brown mare and my father was astride a white horse. Even before we reached the village the farmers started dancing to welcome us. They had even laid out a special and luxuriously appointed cot for me to rest on. There was song and dance and I was fanned with large leaves. It was as if I were a prince.

◆

The idea for the book originated in November 2011, when I wrote an article, which was published in Delhi Gymkhana's *Club Life*, titled *Aam Admi Khas Kahani, Sensex Ki Zubani*. As I work in the financial market, the title felt appropriate. Much like the stock market, my life too has had its share of uncertainty and volatility; in the same vein, living with confidence, determination and willpower, has brought ample rewards.

My book depicts the events that have shaped my life. I had begun life from the lap of luxury, but was, soon, dealt a swift hand and it was fraught with struggles. Eventually, I moved from the footpath to a series of successes.

Beginning with the Partition, the book treads through all the turmoil I witnessed in this country, from the 1940s to the present. The book stands witness to these changes and experiences, and to the changing bonds and values that held it together—from the age of seven till my late seventies. The world has altered drastically: its lifestyles, relationships, priorities and values have undergone many changes.

Through it all, the driving force behind my own thoughts, actions and ambitions has always been to make my children proud. I have wanted them to be able to say out loud, 'Our father achieved this!' That has been my greatest motivation.

I take this opportunity to thank profusely my ever-helpful daughter-in-law Kamakshi Rawal and my darling granddaughter Tejaswi Rawal, who is an Oxfordian, for helping me during the writing process—editing every line of every paragraph and also ensuring the right perspective for the narrative. I would also like to thank Jaideep Krishnan, who did a good job in making the book cohesive. I must mention the efforts put in by Pinkal Kapoor, my office secretary, for typing and re-arranging the manuscript several times to bring it to its present shape.

This story is about an ordinary man: his family, friends, values, memories, best and worst moments, successes and his contentment.

Age	Happiness Sensex
0-7 yrs	51000
7-23yrs	12000
24-26 yrs	25000
27 yrs	7500
28-30 yrs	29000
30 yrs	6000
31-38 yrs	35000
39-48 yrs	45000
49 yrs	3000
51-56 yrs	30000
57 yrs	6000
58-60 yrs	35000
61-70 yrs	47500
71-80 yrs	60000
81-... yrs	

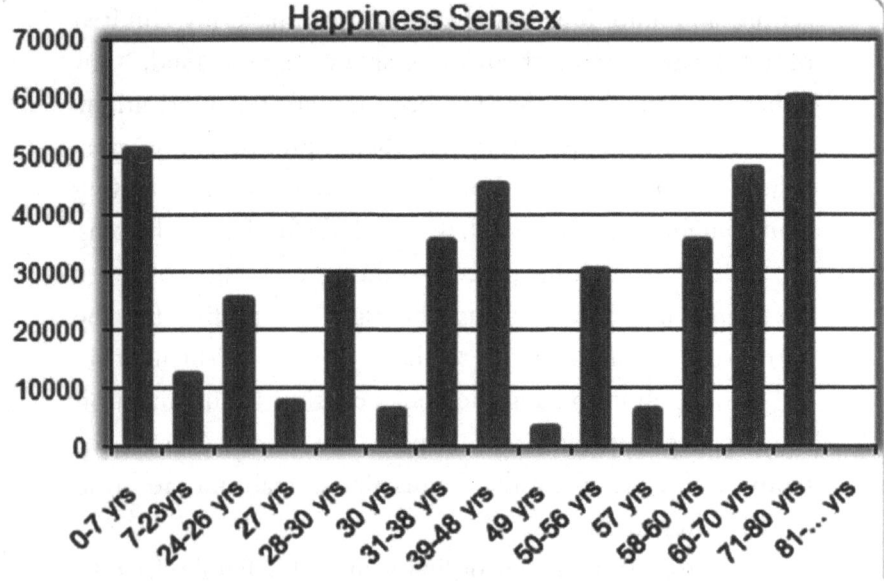

Graph of My Life

PART-I
THE PAST BEATS LIKE A SECOND HEART

1

EARLY YEARS: ABUNDANCE

I was born during one of the coldest nights of the coldest month in Okara, now in Pakistan. I was born into an affluent zamindar family. Most people did not follow the Gregorian calendar, and my mother tells me it was the first day of the month of *Paush*, an very early Sunday morning.

A modern calendar would mark it as the 15th of December, 1940.

The famous film star, Raj Kapoor's birthday is on the 14th of December. I decided to claim the same day as my own birthday as he was my icon those days. The official record, however, states different, and I do not remember how and when that date was decided. I believe that my parents, like many others, approximated a date during the time of my admission into a school.

I was among those privileged to be born with the proverbial silver spoon in their mouth. My father was a famous personality in town. He was closely associated with the Arya

Samaj in Okara and advocated that education be equally available to all children. He even donated the land in front of our own house where the first girls' school of the town was built. My mother was a devotee of the Gurudwara. Though not educated as such, she could recite the Sukhmani Sahib Path from memory. My father was a liberal man and would never object to her faith, he even donated wholeheartedly to the Gurudwara as well.

We were a large family: five brothers and four sisters—a number unimaginable today, but a norm in those days.

Our family lived in a palatial house. Three-storied with six or seven bedrooms, separate studies for each of the children, store rooms where a year's worth of household supplies were stored and cattle sheds manned by a battery of servants. The ground floor was reserved for my father. He would meet guests in the sitting room. They would converse with my father, a traditional hookah[1] kept aside for their pleasure. I was fond of preparing the hookah with tobacco and fire charcoal.

As children, we often went to school riding in a horse-drawn carriage that we owned. I was fond of horse riding, even at the age of five or six. I remember how a particular brown mare would only permit my father or me to ride on her. A keen horse rider himself, my father always kept two horses on the estate. Riding in a horse=drawn carriage, or a horses was a prestigious mode of transport, akin to having a fleet of up-market cars in the garage. Our father preferred

---

[1] A tobacco pipe which draws the smoke through water, contained in a bowl beneath it.

to buy horses which had won tent-pegging[2] contests at a fair or festival.

My father was fond of holding Kabaddi or Dangal matches between all the young children of the mohalla, the area. The kuccha, unpaved, road in front of our house was quite wide and would frequently be dug up to create a kabaddi arena. He would sit with a hookah on a mudha, a cane chair, with a high backrest and ornate arms, watching the matches. At the end of the day's matches, the children would be served hot milk and fruit—preferably bananas.

A buffalo and one cow produced fresh milk for us all. Thrice a week, I used to have a milk bath. I was called Dudhadhari, meaning 'the one who drinks lots of milk'.

Life, for us, was wonderful.

Everything was available in plenty: houses, land, servants, wealth and, to top it all, the repute my father enjoyed in the community. Always dressed in a crisp white shirt and a starched dhoti with a pointed turban (tura), my father cut a majestic figure. His clothes were never washed in the house and always by the city's laundry. During the summers, he would carry a black umbrella. It was said that he was so famed for his punctuality that the people of the town set their clocks by his comings and goings.

---

[2] A daring and skilful sport. A rider on a charging horse uses a lance to pierce and pick up a tent peg on the ground. Success depends on the steadiness of both the rider and the horse.

2

PARTITION: THE STORM WITHIN AND OUTSIDE

During 1945-46 the people of India gathered, filled with fervour for independence, chanting slogans:

Gali Gali Se Aayi Awaaz, Sehgal Dhillon Shahnawaz[3]

Or

O Mera Rang De Basanti Chola... Mai Rang De... Mera Rang De Basanti Chola.[4]

---

[3] The slogan of Netaji's INA (Indian National Army) encapsulating the unity/spirit of India. One Hindu (Sehgal), one Sikh (Dhillon) and one Muslim (Shahnawaz) were Commanders in INA, stressing the unity of all communities.

[4] The clarion call of all independence-seeking revolutionaries, who sought the blessing of their mothers, with a metaphorical request to colour their clothes in Besanti colour (saffron)–the colour of sacrifice.

Or

Bharat Chodo, Azadi Hamara Janam Sidh Adhikar Hai[5]

The Second World War (1937-1944) had just ended, and the winds of change were sweeping across the world. New nations emerged from the shackles of colonial power. The Partition of India in 1947 split British India into two independent nations, India and Pakistan. Partition directly involved the division of three provinces of British India: Assam, Bengal and Punjab, on the basis of a district-level majority of Hindu or Muslim populations.

The boundary dividing India and Pakistan was called the Radcliffe Line [6]. This involved the division of the armed forces of British India, as well as other services between the two new nations, such as the Civil Service, the Railway network and the treasury. British India ceased to exist at midnight on 14–15th August 1947, and two new states of India and Pakistan came into being.

I was just seven at the time of Partition.

As a nation, Pakistan existed as two: West Pakistan and East Pakistan (later Bangladesh in 1971). Though the governments of both, India and Pakistan, announced that people could remain where they were irrespective of religion, the reality on

---

[5] A declaration by Bal Gangadhar Tilak, a great patriot, who gave this call at the Indian National Congress' convocation in Lahore in 1942. 'Leave India – Independence is my birth right.'

[6] The Radcliffe Line was the boundary demarcation line between the Indian and Pakistani portions of the Punjab and Bengal provinces of British India. It was named after its architect, Sir Cyril Radcliffe, who, as the joint chairman of the two boundary commissions for the two provinces, was given the responsibility to divide 175,000 square miles (450,000 km2) of territory with 88 million people.[1]. The demarcation line was published on 17th August 1947 after the Partition of India.

the ground was drastically different. Most Hindus were afraid to stay in Pakistan, and the same fear pervaded the minds of Muslims in India. For their own safety, Hindus in Pakistan and Muslims in India were prompted by their friends and relatives to shift to India and Pakistan, respectively.

Large-scale voluntary and involuntary migration took place across the Radcliffe Line, and millions of Hindus and Muslims were displaced. This shifting of population after the Partition is estimated to be one of the largest human migrations in recorded history. People from all walks of life scrambled for any mode of transport they could find: train, bullock carts, horse carts, camel carts; as a last resort, some went on foot.

This catastrophic migration resulted in a refugee crisis on both sides of the border, marked by large-scale violence. It is estimated that a million people lost their lives in the aftermath of the Partition. This violence continues in the form of a deep-rooted hostility between the people of India and Pakistan, especially in areas directly affected by the violence of those times.

All along the 3,323 kms of the western border, two zones were created: the Pakistan Zone and the Indian Zone—in all the cities, towns and villages in Pakistan. Hindus were shifted to the Indian Zone in each area. In Okara, the division was marked by a straight road beginning from the railway station. Our family was shifted to the Indian Zone. Ironically, this meant that we were staying across the road from our *own* house, which was in the so-called Pakistan Zone. We would sometimes sneak into the Pakistan Zone, even though it was prohibited to visit our home. Despite the upheaval, my father believed that the situation was temporary and that we would eventually return to our house. So firm was he in this belief that, at the time of our leaving the zone, he called my elder brother and me to go to the bazaar to buy strong locks. We locked up the house when we left and gave the keys to him.

Unfortunately, communal riots soon sparked off, affecting the lives of hundreds of thousands of men, women and children, all of whom were mercilessly butchered by raging mobs. I witnessed people panicking, travelling in groups, trying to find a way to get across the border. Some preferred to travel together in caravans, while others felt that the trains would be safer. I personally witnessed horrifying scene at one of the platforms while travelling towards Kurukhestra. I saw few sardarjis carrying a human head on their spearhead and blood was oozing. It was terrible and till date that scene haunts me at times. Also, we read that a train full of corpses was sent from one country to the other.

Memories of Partition

It is said that about 50,000 women were separated from their families. In the province of Punjab alone, around 12 million people were uprooted, and, according to one estimate, almost 20 million people were displaced in the subcontinent. After the Partition, the population of India was around 330 million, and East and West Pakistan had around 30 million people each.

Population of Pakistan

1947: 3.3 Crores	2020: 22.09 Crores
Muslims: 79.7%	Muslims: 96.49%
Hindus:- 13.5%	Hindus: 1.80%
Sikhs: 5.2%	Sikhs: 0.018%
Christians: 1.5%	Christians: 1.10%
Others: 0.1%	Others: 0.42%

Source: https://en.wikipedia.org/wiki/Religion_in_Pakistan

Population of India

1947: 33.00 Crores	2020: 136.65 Crores
Hindu: 84.1%	Hindu: 80.5%
Muslim: 9.8%	Muslim: 14.6%
Christian: 2.3%	Christian: 2.3%
Sikhs: 1.89%	Sikh: 1.9%
Others: 1.91%	Others: 0.42%

https://interviewbubble.com/indian-population-religion-wise-2018-religious-population-in-india/

LEAVING PAKISTAN

Like many other Hindus, our family too, eventually, decided to leave everything behind. We set off for India. A few closely related families decided to join us, looking to my father to make the decisions.

He had to decide our mode of transport.

It was decided that we would travel by train, and all the families were asked to meet at the railway station. When we reached, the platform was overflowing: men, women, children, the elderly and the sick. No fixed time had been stated for the train's arrival. It was not certain whether it would arrive at all. And so, we waited as patiently as we could.

People from all walks of life were at the platform, and everywhere one turned one could see every inch of space taken up. People were sleeping, cooking and even defecating in the open. The platforms had become a theatre. As each train arrived, a mad rush would ensue and people jostled to clamber on to these trains. People would stuff themselves into the carriages, or if they could not find space within, they would perch atop the train and hang from doors, clinging tightly, desperate for whatever foothold they could find.

Our buaji's (father's sister) family was travelling with us. As we waited on the platform, one of buaji's five daughters, who had been engaged a few months earlier, and the prospective groom and his family were also waiting on the same platform. Buaji asked my father for his permission to conduct the wedding ceremony on the platform—immediately—she said that no one knew what destiny had in store—नदी नाम संजोगी मेले। My father agreed.

The marriage was solemnized on the platform with the help of a priest. A makeshift havan kund was assembled with bricks available around, and using branches plucked from the trees nearby as firewood, rituals were performed for the ceremony. I don't remember exactly how the samagri (things required for Havan) was arranged, maybe the Panditji had decided to do away with smagri and did only chanting of mantras—I don't remember. Buaji had been carrying the customary red-coloured attire for the bride and a little jewellery on her person.

After what seemed like a never-ending wait, a train arrived. Everyone rushed to enter the carriages. Our buaji's family boarded the train, as did our family. However, my eldest sister, Lajwanti, refused to leave without her husband, who had not yet arrived from his village, and she disembarked. My mother echoed my sister's sentiments and said that if her daughter would not go, she would not either, and thus our plan was abandoned.

Our family returned to our makeshift house in the Indian Zone. Whether fate or divine intervention, I cannot say, but this act saved us; we were later told that most of the passengers on that ill-fated train were massacred, including the newlywed bride and groom and their families.

After we had returned from the station, it was decided that we would join a caravan. The caravan we joined consisted of some 1000-1200 people, crowded into about a hundred bullock carts. Most people hired or bought bullock carts, and four or five families shared each bullock cart. My father, who owned land in four villages and many bulls, cows, buffaloes, and bullock carts, was helpless.

All our livestock remained in the villages and, as almost

everybody working the fields was Muslim, we did not dare travel into those areas. Our carts were not returned to us. Ultimately, we had to buy a bullock cart from the market. Two bulls and a cart cost us a princely sum and we shared it with four other families.

My father, as the nominal head of the families, asked everyone to carry as little baggage as possible. At the back of his mind, he still believed we would return soon and he gave strict instructions to my mother to not carry anything unnecessary. We would only carry two trunks of valuables among the ten of us in the family. My mother secretly entrusted my eldest brother with a few coins and he hid it under the cart in a small wooden box meant for axle-grease.

It was a two-day journey to the Indian border town of Fazilka, some 70 or 80 kilometres away. We would have to walk the entire distance. Only my younger sister and brother, five and three years old respectively, could be accommodated in the cart itself. They would sit atop the mounds of baggage. For security, two Gorkha soldiers rode on horses, that patrolled up and down on each side of the caravan. Some of the caravan members were also carrying their own guns, most of them twelve-bore double-barreled guns.

The journey itself was a horrifying experience: we were attacked en route, and the scorching heat of August took its toll on everybody. Water was scarce. The caravan stopped for water at ponds and lakes, common water sources for villages. At one place, where the caravan stopped for water near a village, what we witnessed chilled us to the bone. A buffalo had been butchered and thrown into the pond. To avoid dying of thirst, people were drawing the bloody water from as far away from the buffalo as possible, filtering it through cloth, and keeping it aside so that the blood would sediment, and they could drink the water that floated atop.

When we arrived at the station, we came across many apparent sympathizers whose intentions and motives were unknown. One person approached us, and helped to place our luggage in the train. We later found that the man had stolen a sewing machine belonging to my eldest sister, some clothes belonging to buaji, as well as a few utensils.

We reached Fazilka but it was overcrowded, and our family decided to shift to one of the refugee camps. Since most of us wanted to be far from the border, we decided on the camp at Kurukshetra.

I have realized that in the darkest of hours, in the most desperate of times, humanity still triumphs. Something occurs to restore our faith. Though I was too young to remember it, one such incident is worth recounting.

On that ill-fated train from Okara that I mentioned earlier, we knew another family. They were my future sister-in-law's elder sister and her in-laws and they were aboard that train. Raj had been married for about a year and a half and had a child, two or three months old. When the train was stopped and attacked, she witnessed the murder of her husband and his family. She managed to jump out of the train and hide herself and her son under the train. The baby was wailing, and she tried to quiet him by placing her hand over his mouth. Scared, she ran and hid behind the bushes along the track.

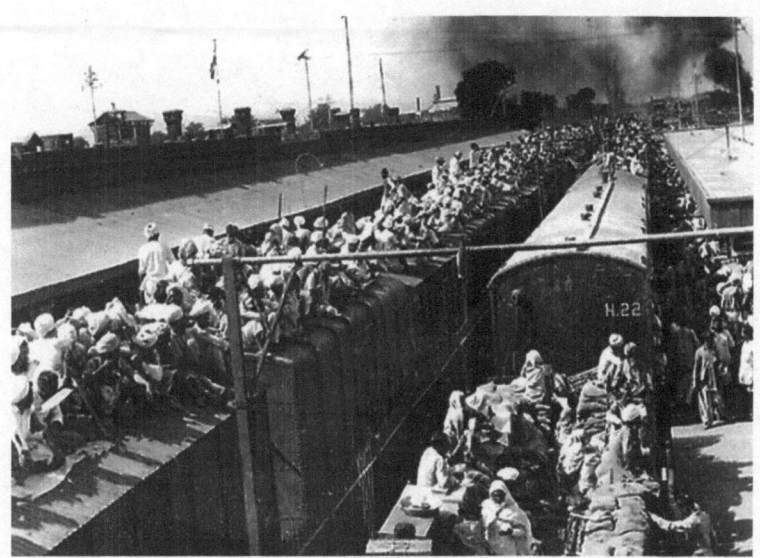

Memories of Partition

An elderly Muslim gentleman, witnessing her predicament, came up to her and said, 'Daughter, your baby's cries will eventually reach the ears of these butchers, and you can very well imagine ... If you can trust me, come with me. I have two daughters and we will keep you safe and get you to India.'

With no alternative, she went with him. This gentleman gave her safe passage to India, and he even looked through different refugee camps at Jallandhar and Ambala, and safely brought her to us at Kurukshetra. When I think upon it now that I'm older, the story restores my faith in humanity; reminding me that people of character and integrity, transcending caste, creed, and religion, are everywhere.

3

RE-STARTING FROM ZERO

Management of this sea of humanity at the camps was a stupendous task for the nations. Different areas in India were allotted to natives of specific districts from Pakistan, and they were asked to settle in temporary camps.

After a long trek out of Pakistan through Punjab, our family arrived at the refugee camp at Kurukshetra, the very site where Lord Krishna delivered his sermon to Arjuna in the *Bhagavat Gita*; the site of the epic battle described in the *Mahabharata*.

Many refugees remained in the camp for more than a year. Having lost everything, the little they received as free ration and accommodation were dear to them. The camp distributed free rations, blankets and sometimes it came with powdered milk; my father was not used to such fare. My elder brother and I would walk a few kilometers every day for fresh milk, making sure our father received the curd he was so fond of.

Prime Minister Jawaharlal Nehru at the Kurukshetra refugee camp in April 1948. Originally intended for 100,000 people, the number soon swelled to thrice that.

We were forced into a situation so radically different from the lifestyle we were used to. If I have to describe that scene at refugee camp vis-e-vis our life style at Okara one could say, in a single word, the difference was like heaven and earth. There were hundreds of tents in the camp, erected side-by-side. No facilities—no amenities per se. Drinking Water—one tap per around 50-100 tents (sometime we had to walk about a kilometre to get a bucket of water from a nearby village well). No electricity in the tent. Streets were lit from temporary erected poles at distances. And worst of all, no sanitation facilities. Men would go to the open fields to relieve themselves. For the women, there were makeshift community lavatories made of rough jute screens, erected around dug-up earth, sometime even the jute clothing would be torn. The bathing areas were communal. Living in a tent, sleeping on the bare uneven rough floor, crammed with everybody inside was a tough call.

My father who was used to his aristocratic lifestyle had to adjust to the change. My mother too, who had had a battery of servants, had to do everything by herself including the cleaning/maintaining of the floor. Of course, my brothers and sisters would lend a hand in this daily course.

One day, my mother was cooking food in a vessel, but since she did not have a stirring spoon, she stirred with the branch of a tree. A lady, who would later become my elder brother's mother-in-law, was passing by. Noticing my mother, the lady remarked in Punjabi, '*Shahni, adhe shahar di malak ho ke dal de vaste tere kol kadchi vi nahin?*' (O rich lady, you once owned almost half of the city, and you don't even have a proper spoon to stir your food?) She returned soon after with a spoon for my mother.

But I do believe the herd community has its own positive effect, when you see everyone around suffering—your pain become bearable. Luckily, and thanks to our parents training, everybody in the family accepted the reality and moved on.

As the old proverb goes, 'what cannot be cured must be endured,' and people from all walks of life whether rich zamindars or simple workers, all had to adjust to these circumstances.

Shifting to Kaithal

We stayed at Kurukshetra in tented accommodations for almost half a year, until we finally decided to shift. My father was against staying in the refugee camp for too long and he persuaded our relatives to find us somewhere to shift to. One of our relatives knew a prominent advocate in Kaithal Tehsil, now a district, about 50 kilometres from Kurukshetra. My father, with a few others, set out for Kaithal. In Kaithal, they sought the advocate, Amar Nath Tiwari, a renowned personage of the city. A man who would later become a member of the Punjab Legislative Council.

Mr Tiwari received my father and the others with warmth and asked how he could be of help. The four expressed their desire to shift to and settle in Kaithal. Tiwari was pleased, and he told them that many Muslim families had left the city for Pakistan, locking up their houses just as our family had done while leaving for India. Tiwari advised all of them to look around the city and locate locked houses such as theirs. When they found suitable houses, they could break the lock and occupy the houses. They could then inform him of the address, so that the houses could be officially allotted to them.

This arrangement may appear strange to a reader today, but I believe this was the norm immediately following Partition, on both sides of the border. I also believe houses would not have been allotted for nothing. One had to prove ownership back in Pakistan and thus would be finally allotted in lieu of that. My father had brought papers outlining his ownership of property in Pakistan.

My father selected a modest but well-located house with two floors and a huge veranda, as well as space to house a couple of cows or horses. It was perfect for the family.

4

JOYS OF CHILDHOOD

I have always been a restless person, and even at the young age of seven, I could not sit idle in the refugee camp. There was no school and the government had declared that all children who had come as refugees would be promoted to the next class without sitting for an exam.

My cousin brother, my very dear Kahan Chand and I, sold homemade sweets on the railway platform nearby. Each day, my buaji would prepare sweets of rice and jaggery and place them neatly in an iron box. Kahan Chand would bring them to the platform where I would join him. We also bought cigarettes of a variety of brands from the market, bidis (unprocessed tobacco wrapped in leaves) and machis (a match box) and sold them on the platform to eager passengers.

We were both about the same age, Kahan Chand was only a month older than I and we enjoyed our task. We also earned money. Buaji would hand over some of our earnings to me, and I gave them to my mother when I returned home to our tent.

It was not always an easy task. Once, a customer, sitting on the roof of a railway coach, asked Kahan Chand to throw a packet of cigarettes up to him. Kahan Chand did. But with the pack in his hand, the passenger refused to throw down the money owed to us. He put out a thumb and mocked us. We were young and unused to such treatment and Kahan Chand began to cry. I devised another plan. I immediately began to shout for justice and attracted a crowd of people. The crowds began scolding the man, and he was forced to pay up.

A train scene akin to those my cousin, Kahan Chand and I experienced while selling homemade sweets and cigarettes

In Kaithal, to make ends meet, my father opened a grocery shop. What a change for a man who had been living in luxury! The shop was an avenue of adventures for me. I was given the fascinating duty of selling sugar. The rate was about 8-12 paisa per seer (0.93 kilogram). The sugar was kept in an open mound, known as a dheri, on an empty jute bag. There was no weighing machine as such. I would weigh the sugar on a scale with a wooden rod to balance it; two plates held the weights on one side and sugar on the other. I enjoyed this immensely. Unfortunately, due to government regulations and controls, the shop had to be closed.

My mother was simple, pious and brave. She was also extremely resourceful. She often asked my elder sister and me to collect cow/buffalo dung after school ended, as the cattle would return after the day's grazing around the same time. We would wait for their signal— their raised tails—and then rush to collect the dung by placing our iron vessels beneath their rear. We had been warned not to tell our father about this lest it hurt his pride, but we ourselves took great pride in supplementing our family's income. My mother made cow dung cakes, put them in the sun and once they had dried, used half of them as firewood for cooking in the house and sold the rest.

The family too was growing. My eldest brother, Dayal Chandji, was married. He had been engaged as a child, and the girl's family was keen on having the marriage solemnized soon during those uncertain times. Marriages were often fixed between families before the children were born. My father, and a close friend of his, both wanted to cement their friendship into a familial bond and they had decided.

Had things been normal, my father would have insisted that all of us keep studying. We could even go abroad, to England, for higher studies. But our circumstances had changed so drastically that he had to change the plans and priorities. After the grocery shop was forcibly shut and once my eldest brother got married, two of my older brothers, Dayal Chandji and Roshan Lalji, were sent to Nilokheri. Nilokheri was a new satellite town near Karnal district, which had been created to help refugees from West Pakistan to develop skills. The two were to learn technical skills & earn, providing the family with a new source of income.

Nilokheri was about 60 kilometres away, and one had to take two trains to reach there. My eldest brother had learnt book-binding as a hobby in school; he applied for a job as a book-binding Master (teacher) in Nilokheri. He was offered a job at a salary of 30 rupees per month, out of which the newlywed couple sent two-thirds back to our parents. This helped us run the household at Kaithal.

Roshan Lalji was good at painting, and he got the opportunity to learn from a great teacher, Mr Subramaniam, who was once a royal painter in the kingdom of Baroda. My brother, later, became a very good painter, creating imaginative scenes rapidly. After he was fully trained, both the brothers went to Delhi, where they opened a shop: 'Zathapat Phatafat Painters' (or instant painters) in Pahar Ganj market. I have often felt that Roshan Lalji was as talented as M.F. Hussain, Raja Ravi Varma or S. H. Raza, and would have reached their heights had he continued in the same profession and pursued it with single-minded dedication. But, as they say, hunger comes first, and he had to work to earn money for the family and himself.

At that time, Nilokheri was a jungle—infested with snakes—and my brother and bhabhi lived in a tent, exposed to all sorts of perils. I had seen monkeys catching snakes on the road, killing them by thrashing their heads against the coal tar road. Once in a while, a snake would catch and kill a monkey too.

I travelled to Nilokheri every Saturday to deliver food my mother had cooked, enough to last my brothers two or three days. Eight years old, and I would board a train all alone, changing tracks at Kurukshetra to reach Nilokheri. I would return at night by the same train, reaching Kaithal at 10 p.m.

During one of these journeys back to Kaithal, an incident took place. I still shudder to recall it. I had fallen asleep and missed my stop. The train continued its journey and finally stopped at the last station, Jind Junction. As the passengers began to disembark, I was still fast asleep. A man woke me up and told me that the train had passed Kaithal two hours ago. Tears welled up in my eyes—what was I to do? Just then, a couple approached me. They consoled me, and told me that they would help me board a train to Kaithal.

I was taken to the side of the platform and we sat on a deserted bench. Saying they would return in a few minutes, they left me to wait by myself. A gentleman—I would rather call him a devta; a god in human form—had been watching us. He caught me by the hand and began to scold me.

'Do you know what this couple could have done to you?'

I learnt that it was common, those days, for children to be kidnapped and maimed, left to become beggars. According to the gentleman, this couple had the same intention.

He picked me up and put me aboard a train that was ready to leave for Kaithal. He requested that the passengers help me reach Kaithal safely, and they did. *The experience still sends a shiver up my spine whenever I recall it.*

5

LEARNINGS FROM KAITHAL

In Kaithal, I joined a primary school in Class III. I don't remember whether I studied much during the time I spent there but I did spend a lot of time playing—that was between 1947-49.

1950-55, my time in high school, was the best period of my youth. I was an all-rounder at school. In Class X, I was even honoured as a school captain and then as a general monitor. While I was an average student when it came to academics, but I played almost every sport: hockey, football, badminton, ring, kabaddi and even basketball. I excelled at basketball and hockey and was made the vice-captain of the basketball team and captain of the hockey team. My team and I played matches all across the district, even at the state level.

My family was supportive of my athletic abilities. Whenever I played an important match, my father or my brothers would come from Delhi, just to cheer me. They became a source of inspiration for the team, as they lavishly distributed prizes and sweets when we achieved victories.

I was also fond of declamation contests and my father encouraged my participation. I was comfortable speaking in public and was asked by the headmaster to address the whole school, comprising about 1000 students, every morning. I read daily newspaper headlines. It was a great feeling to speak in front of so many students. To this day, I continue to enjoy speaking to a crowd.

On one occasion, the Municipal Committee arranged a function to commemorate the martyrdom of Vir Haqiqat Rai (the twelve-year-old martyr who had been executed in 1736) on Vasant Panchami Day. Hundreds had gathered on the school grounds and I was asked to speak. I had rehearsed well and I spoke powerfully and sensitively. After the speech, many people congratulated my father and blessed me. It was a wonderful feeling to be so felicitated.

Our school administration was strict and disciplinarian, and punishment was often meted rather out liberally for both actual and imagined offences. Once, after I had received good marks in a test, a teacher accused me of cheating from another student. Despite my denying it, he refused to accept it as the truth. He insisted, and as punishment, declared that I would receive ten blows from a wooden stick on each hand. I asserted myself. Firstly, I told him that I had not cheated, and secondly, said that if he was so determined to punish me, I would accept ten strokes on one wrist alone. The whole class was aghast. Nobody had before dared to defy the teacher. Students watched as I received those strokes, my hand becoming swollen and red. Much later, the teacher realized his error and apologized—not directly—but in a message conveyed through another teacher.

During school, among many other activities, I was very fond of cycling and horse riding. However, I was also fond of watching movies, which my father did not approve of. Negotiating with my father, I told him that if he bought me a new cycle, I would not go to the movies. And so, he bought me a brand-new green-coloured Raleigh cycle—a Premium Brand. Thus, for a month or so, I did not watch movies at all. Eventually, the urge resurfaced, though it had subdued.

For a month or so, I rode my brand-new bicycle everywhere, ringing the bell continuously to attract the attention of passersby, showing off my new cycle and the bright coloured clothes I would wear. It was such fun. I even joined a school boys' cycle rally to Ambala, which was about 80 kilometres away. It was a fantastic ride; we cycled along the banks of rivers and through green fields.

Now, as a movie buff, I often recall the instance where my blind passion for watching movies changed the entire course of my life. I was then fifteen years old. I was fascinated by the lifestyle within the army and joined the NCC (National Cadet Corps), the Army-managed youth wing. I passed with an 'A' certificate. In those days, one had to clear a written exam and then pass the SSB (Service Selection Board) interview for JSW (Joint Services Wing) to join the Army as an officer. I cleared the written exam and was called for the SSB at Meerut, but for a cause I no longer remember, I missed it. I wrote a letter to the Defence Ministry about missing the SSB and requested a second chance. I was informed that since the JSW's SSB was closed, they could accommodate me with the Indian Military Academy (IMA) candidates. I agreed and left for the SSB at Bangalore. After all tests ended, an officer who introduced himself as Major Kapur, personally informed me that I had been selected. However, when I looked at the list of successful candidates, my name was missing. I approached Major Kapur, who told me that someone else had been selected due to pressures from within the Army Headquarters.

Not one to give up, I appeared again for the same exam the next year, passed it, and was called for the SSB at Meerut. My father knew the CO (Commanding Officer) at the SSB Meerut, and he decided to accompany me to Meerut. The train departed from Kaithal at 5 a.m. the next day.

My father was in the habit of going to bed early; as we had to leave early, he told me to go to bed early too. I agreed and lay down on the cot, on the roof of the house.

But I could not sleep. I was excited to go to Meerut, and thoughts of joining the Army accumulated. Unable to sleep, my old habit reared its head, and I thought of watching a movie—*Samadhi*, starring Ashok Kumar and Nalini Jaywant—at the theatre nearby. Quietly, I went downstairs and informed my mother. Despite her cautioning that I should not to even consider going to the theatre at such an hour and that my father would not like it, I prevailed upon her to manage the situation. I would not be able to sleep anyway from sheer excitement. My mother reluctantly agreed and I sneaked away gleefully.

Unfortunately, it so happened that my elder brother, Roshan Lalji, arrived unannounced from Delhi at about 10 p.m. that night. My parents woke up and the three of them sat talking for a while. My father asked my mother to call me downstairs as I would not be able to meet my brother the next day. My mother tried to cover up my absence, stating

I should not be disturbed, that I had just slept and so on, but my father grew suspicious and demanded to know the truth. On learning that I had disobeyed him, my father grew furious and refused to accompany me for the journey.

When I returned from the movie, around 1 a.m., my mother opened the door quietly and told me everything; if I wanted to go to Meerut the next day, I would have to go on my own. I was not to disturb my father. And though I did go to Meerut by myself, I could not get through the SSB, and never applied again.

Maybe I was not destined to serve the Indian Army. In retrospect, when I think back on the years that followed, I think of thousands of young officers who died in the wars against China and Pakistan. I could have been one of them. But the lesson I learnt, from the above episode, was very loud and clear: He who pays the piper, calls the tune.

College Days

My father wanted me to continue studying after school. He desired that I, unlike my brothers, should be the first in my generation to graduate from college. To be a graduate those days was a big deal.

In 1955, I passed my Matriculation Exam and joined as an FSc (Fellow of Science) student at RKSD College, Kaithal. Going to college was a matter of pride. My time in college was spent well, but not wisely. I continued to play sports, participate in dramas and socialize. I was even known as a show-off, a braggart. I remember a campfire organised by the college; the Deputy Commissioner from Karnal had arrived as the chief guest. I was to perform a song on stage—'Mera juta hai Japani' from the movie *Shree 420*. To imitate Raj Kapoor perfectly, I bought a new pair of shoes and made a hole in them with a blade, hoping to resemble his tattered fleet shoes and slightly-short trousers, much to my father's amusement.

Participating in every other extracurricular activity took its toll and my academic performance was affected badly. During my final preparatory exams, my performance was pathetic, and I received a zero in physics! My professors refused to let me fill out the form for the university exams as I had not met the minimum cut-off marks.

With only a month-and-a-half left, I told my father the truth. I assured him that I had the capacity and capability to study hard and clear the final exams. Initially, he refused and asked me to study another year seriously before I tried again, but I persuaded my mother to prevail upon him. I wanted to pass the same year.

Reluctantly, he agreed; he made it very clear that though he would accompany me to the Principal's office, he would not argue on my behalf. But I was certain that my father could make things go my way. And that is exactly what happened.

It was winter. Accompanying me was my father, dressed in the typical garb of a well-to-do landlord of the time: a white Punjabi dhoti, a white shirt, white turban with projected turra, a fan-shaped crest, and bleached white starched shiny black pathani shoes. By this time, my father had become an influential person in the city, both as a landowner and a philanthropist. People in the city respected him. He was greeted respectfully by all in the college and was taken straight to the Principal's office.

I remember the scene as if it were yesterday: my father facing the Principal across the table; I, standing just behind him. The Principal told my father that my appearing for the exam would be a waste of money and would lower the reputation of the college. My father then turned to me. I promised my father and the Principal that in the little time I had left, I would study hard and that I would clear the exams. Seeing my determination, my father told the Principal to forward the application.

It was a do-or-die situation. I hardly slept during the remaining one and a half months. A separate room was allotted to me, and nobody was permitted to disturb me. I don't remember what I ate, even though my mother would often bring me something or the other, quietly. I was literally burning the midnight oil, and challenging myself.

To everybody's immense surprise, I passed the exams. My physics professor, Mr Thussu, had earlier declared that if I could pass, everybody else in the university would too. To my glee and his utter dismay, four of his favourite students failed. When I graduated in 1959, my father's desire to see at least one of his sons graduate from college was fulfilled, making him extremely happy.

Around the same time, an interesting incident occurred. I have always been fascinated by royal families. In the year 1959, I read in the newspaper that the Duke of Edinburgh (who expired recently on 9th April, 2021 at his ripe age of 99) would be attending the Republic Day parade in New Delhi. Though he was the husband of the Queen—the monarch—people perceived him as the King of England. I wanted to see him and, more than that, I wanted to see what kind of clothes he wore. I was staying with my brothers in Delhi and asked them if they were interested in witnessing the parade. As they were busy with work, I decided to go alone.

I was so excited that on the 25th of January, I asked my brothers if I could watch a movie at night; I would walk to Rajpath from there. They laughed at my enthusiasm and let me go. In the severely cold month of January, I left wearing nothing but a sweater and a woolen blanket over my kurta-pajama. The cold did not seem to matter. After the movie at Odeon cinema hall, I walked all the way to Rajpath and found a cement bench right in front of the podium. There was barely any security and I slept on the bench, not wanting to miss even a glimpse of the 'King'.

I woke around 5 a.m. and selected my vantage point: a tree right opposite the stage, across the road. I sat comfortably upon a branch, awaiting the events with bated breath. The hustle and bustle began around 7 a.m. and soon the place filled with people. Gradually the dignitaries began to arrive. Finally, Prime Minister, Jawaharlal Nehru arrived with the Duke of Edinburgh, followed by the President of India, Rajendra Prasad in a spectacular horse carriage. After his arrival, the national anthem was played, and the three-hour parade began. I watched it comfortably on the branch, enjoying every second. I don't think anybody ever enjoyed watching the Republic Day Parade as much as I did that day.

Immediately after the parade, the President of India left. I saw Jawaharlal Nehru and the Duke of Edinburgh standing together. I quickly climbed off the tree, and rushed across the road to the stage where they stood. I greeted the Prime Minister with a namaste, and then reached out and touched the back of the Duke. I wasn't trying to be rude; I just wanted to know what kind of cloth the suit was made of. It was a camel-coloured gabardine suit. The Duke turned to me and shook my hand, and I was on cloud nine.

Years later, when I bought my first suit, it was, of course, a camel-coloured gabardine.

6

MOONLIGHTING IN COLLEGE

Three incidents have changed the course of my life. I've already mentioned the first. The second happened around the same time as well. As I prepared to join the armed forces, I had joined a coaching institution: S.N. Das Gupta College in Delhi. During the day, I went to the coaching college, after which I would work at my brothers' business.

My fees for the coaching college and the evening classes, and my other expenses were rather high, especially when compared to expenses of my brother's household. Right from my early years, I am very fond of entertaining friends—makes me a feel good and brings me happiness—but that results in extra expenses. My eldest brother, with whom I was staying, was uncomfortable with this but did not say anything. He wrote a letter to my father at Kaithal, detailing the comparative expenses: for two months my personal expenses amounted to Rupees 427/-, compared to the total expense of the rest of the household—including both the brothers, their wives and two children—which was Rupees 209/- only. My brother requested father that I should be either called back to the village or that the expenses should be borne by my father.

Comparative Expenses Statement–Mine verses family

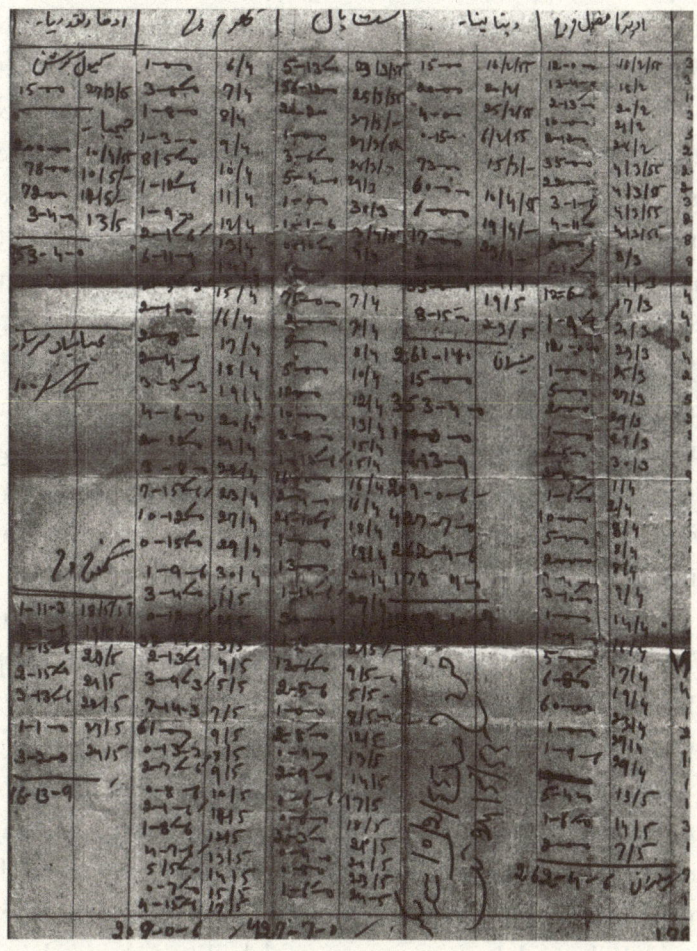

As chance would have it, I reached Kaithal on one of my usual visits, the day after this letter reached my father.

I remember being so excited to meet my parents that I had called out my arrival from the street. My mother welcomed me and called me upstairs to partake in lunch. However, instead of immediately going upstairs, I entered the drawing room on the ground floor. I saw an envelope lying atop the radio and I recognized the handwriting of my eldest brother. Curiosity overcame my manners, and I opened the letter and read it.

The words had an electrifying effect on me. I immediately felt that I was not welcome in my brother's house, and doubted his love for me. Placing the letter in my pocket, I walked upstairs in a daze, and informed my mother that I needed to go back to Delhi as I had remembered something very urgent.

She was perplexed. She began to plead with me to stay; my sisters pleaded me to at least have lunch. But I insisted. I rushed to the bus station and boarded the first available bus for Delhi. Though I reached Delhi by 6 p.m., I did not go to my brother's house. Instead, I visited an old schoolmate living in Darya Ganj, who had started a job with the State Bank of India.

I spent the evening with him without disclosing anything. We went for a movie, but my thoughts were disturbed. I kept thinking about my options. I did not want to go where I was deemed a burden. Why should I go if I was unwanted?

After the movie, my friend insisted that I stay the night, but I excused myself. I left by 1 a.m. and started walking. I reached Connaught Place, deciding I would not go to the house and would instead sleep somewhere else. But where would I sleep? I had no money and had never stayed in a hotel or a dharamshala. I did not know where to go.

I decided I would sleep on the footpath. I slept on the wooden porch of a shop, Jayna Photo Studio, in CP. I had commissioned a portrait of my father (which I still have) from this very shop. I slept soundly, and the next morning I woke up determined. I set off to find a job. I got two jobs, both offering a meagre sum of rupees 70 per month.

I still have the appointment letters.

My First Job Appointement Letter

WELDON SALES CORPORATION
PAHARGANJ BRIDGE
NEW DELHI

Ref. No. _____ Dated 21-10-57

Letter of appointment.

Name of the Establishment.	Weldon Sales Corporation.
Address:	Original Road, Paharganj Bridge, NewDelhi
Name of the employee.	Shri Sat Pal.
Father's name	Malik Pearey Lal Rawal.
Address.	43- Basti Harphul Singh.
The hour of work.	8 (eight hours.)
Date of appointment.	21-10-1957.
Rate of wages or salary.	70/- (Rs. Seventy only) Per Month.
Designation or nature of work.	Clerk 3 months probation period (Temporary.)
Other concessions or benefits, if any that may be special to his appointment.	NO.
Signature of employee.	For Weldon Sales Corporation.
(Sd.) Dated 21/10/1957. Sat Pal Rawal	Managing Proprietor.

The first offer was from a dry-cleaner's shop, which I accepted. I put the appointment letter in my pocket and began to walk towards the house I had stayed in for so long. In my heart of hearts, I did not want to work in a dry-cleaning shop. Still undecided, I was walking down the road and saw the board of the Weldon Sales Corporation. 'Manufacturers of Ink and Gum' it said. I had used their ink before and I felt some sort of familiarity. I walked in to ask about a job. Luckily for me, the owner, S. Harnam Singh, was there. He met me, took a typing test, and appointed me as typist-cum-dispatch clerk. I happily took the appointment letter and reached home.

At home, I met my brother, and very respectfully, I announced that I had gotten a job. I would not take any money from their house. He was perplexed, surprised and shocked. He did not know why I was acting in this manner.

In retrospect, I realized that I had been too hasty and irrational. My brother had informed our father of the comparative expenses. Obviously, my expenses were not justifiable, and now I feel my brother was right to inform the head of the family. Maybe there was rebellion within me which prompted me to take the step that I did. Looking back, I think it was a blessing in disguise to make me feel independent and confident. I have never, till this day, disclosed the background to any of my brothers; not even to my father till his last breath.

I now had a new daily routine, starting from waking up at 6.30-7 a.m., getting ready, and cycling off to the office by 8.30 a.m. I would carry my tiffin, which was tied to the carrier of my cycle. I would work the whole day, and at 6 p.m. rush to the evening college and study till 10 p.m. I had joined the evening college to complete my graduation and fulfil my father's desire. When I would reach home, my dinner would be kept aside for me in a thali (a large plate).

I would take it to the roof and eat it there, studying by the light of a lantern. I kept to this routine for months.

Almost half a year into the job, the owner called for me and handing me a cloth duster, told me to clean his car. I mechanically took the duster and walked up to his car. The moment I placed the duster on the roof of the car, my inner-self revolted.

Did I need the job so desperately that I would clean the owner's car, like a servant?

In a flash I decided to quit. I picked up my cycle from outside the office and left, the duster still in my hands. I had left my tiffin behind in my haste. I told my brother that I had left the job, without disclosing the reason. He was overjoyed and glad to have me back in his fold.

The owner had waited for me to return before he began his search. Having found my brother, he inquired with him about my leaving. He even offered to double my salary and add some perks, but I refused. My brother supported my decision.

7

WORK AND MARRIAGE: A NEW PHASE

After a while in Delhi, I started looking for a job again. I wanted to be independent. I appeared for many competitive exams and was finally selected for the post of a clerk with Life Insurance Corporation of India (LIC) of India in 1958.

When I joined LIC, my pay totalled 130 rupees per month. When I look back, I realize what every *paisa* meant those days. A clause in my employment contract noted that if I completed my graduation, I would get an increment of Rupees 10 per month, which immensely motivated me. Another clause stated an increment of same amount if I also took on the role of a cashier. I opted for it.

```
                                LIFE INSURANCE
                                CORPORATION OF INDIA
        ─────────────────────────────────────────────────
               NORTHERN ZONAL OFFICE:    Post Box No. 160,
                                         Lakshmi Insurance Building,
                                         Asaf Ali Road, NEW DELHI.
        Ref. Secretarial &                      18 OCT 1958
             Personnel.
        ─────────────────────────────────────────────────

             Shri Sat Pal Rawal,
             Rawal Painting House,
             43, Basti Harphool Singh, Sadar Thana Road, Delhi.6.
             Sadar Thana Road, Delhi-6.
             Dear Sir,
                      With reference to your application dated 26.8.1958
             you are hereby offered the post of an Assistant in the scale
             of Rs.75-5-90-6-120-8-136-EB-8-160-10-220-EB-10-240-15-270.
             Your initial pay shall be Rs.75.00 per month during the proba-
             tionary period.
```

I completed my graduation in 1959. I had a permanent job and a graduate degree, both. I was barely twenty-one when people began to approach my parents with marriage proposals for me. In our house, our eldest sister's words were respected as the last word in any family matter. While at her in-laws, my sister had noticed Krishna. She discussed and finalized everything with Krishna's family and sent a postcard to my father—it stated that she had seen and liked the girl and finalized my marriage. She did say that if we had any objection, the girl's family would have to be told by my parents. Back then, once the eldest sister had agreed, nobody in the family went against her word. Nevertheless, times were changing, and my parents and brothers wanted me to have some say in the matter.

Krishna, along with another lady, was called to our house on some vague pretext. When they reached our home, I was called from the office. I was not keen on getting married and tried to find an excuse, but my family members declared that I must at least see the girl. I confided in my friend in the office, and we came up with a plan. He ruffled my hair, making it seem disheveled and dirtied my shirt. We hoped it would make a bad impression on the girl, and she would reject me herself.

I cycled home, and by the time I reached, I was trembling. I felt as if I were committing a sin by looking at a girl. I was confused and I wondered how I would feel if, someday, someone declined to marry any one of my sisters.

I climbed the stairs to our home on the first floor with great difficulty. I was trembling when my sister-in-law saw me at the entrance and asked me to come in. She sensed my hesitation, and gently asked me to fetch two cokes. I rushed downstairs on that pretext and brought two cola bottles up. I was very uncomfortable sitting in the room, even though it only lasted a few moments. I did not know what to say, nor had the courage to ask anything. I think I had barely caught a glimpse of Krishna's face before I almost ran out.

My brothers were waiting downstairs. I told them that I wasn't sure; I had barely glimpsed her. I didn't think she had seen me either. My brothers asked whether I disliked her, to which I said 'No'. That was all. My brothers declared that if I didn't dislike her, it meant I had no objection, and Bahenji—our eldest sister—had already agreed.

My wedding was fixed.

The Wedding

The wedding date was finalized. 11 May 1961. Until we were married, there were to be no phone calls, no letters exchanged, no movies or meetings. I would first speak to Krishna when we were married.

My younger sister's wedding was also finalized around the same date. Hers was solemnized on 5 May 1961. This was the norm, especially in Punjabi families, that in the case of two marriages in the house, the daughter's wedding would take place first. Invitation cards were sent out with both our names on it. Another card was designed by my brother and printed at Delhi, which announced only my wedding. I have kept both these cards with me still, over all t hese years.

During my sister's wedding, we had to arrange for a mare for the groom to ride, in the procession. My father had arranged with a mahant[7] to lend us his mare for the day. I was asked to fetch a mare from the dera[8]. My father warned me to not give in to the temptation of riding the mare, who was known to be a ferocious creature; I was to simply hold the reins and walk her home.

I arrived at the dera and climbed on to the mare's back, guiding her slowly out of the stables. I was riding a horse after a long time and felt euphoric. Instead of tracing my footsteps back to the house, I took her to a huge ground just outside the city limits and let the reins fall free. It was

---

[7]The head of a religious sect
[8]The abode of a mahant is called a dera.

as if the mare had been waiting for this very opportunity: she ran across the ground at breakneck pace. It seemed like she was floating on air. Onlookers appeared flabbergasted at our speed and pace.

I don't remember how many rounds we rode together. But her speed was terrifying. She was sweating, but she seemed to enjoy herself. I was happy and unfazed about the consequences.

After what seemed like half an hour, I remembered the task I had set out on and decided to slow down the mare. I pulled at the reins, but she just would not stop. I felt that she sped up instead and it scared me a bit. I turned the horse towards the city, hoping that she would slow down in front of a crowd but it was in vain.

Anything could happen. I wanted to avoid an accident and had to stop her. Instantly, and with great difficultly, I jumped off the saddle and wrapped my arms around her neck. With all my weight around her neck she slowed, and eventually stopped. It was one of the most thrilling experiences of my life. Here I was, a prospective groom, clinging to a horse! When I think back, the risks had been great, but who was scared at that age?

In the year 1961, I was twenty-one and Krishna, my wife, was sixteen. My father-in-law was the sarpanch of a village called 50GG in Bikaner in Sri Gangapur district. One had to take three different trains and a bus to get there for the marriage. Half the marriage party travelled on the roof of the bus. They were warned about overhanging branches of thorny trees, and headgear was advised. What an experience it was! The bus tilted in its speed, moving from one side to the other, and sandstorms blew strong. For those on the roof, it felt like eating mud.

When we arrived, we were accommodated in the primary school at the village. As we were on our way to the bride's house, another sandstorm blew, followed by a thunderstorm so fierce it felt like a hurricane. We had to remain seated on the cots, covering ourselves in the dark, waiting for the storm to die down so we could go ahead with the rituals.

We were served food during the storm in a hilarious manner. The groom's family all sat atop the cots. As we were all covered with kesh (light blankets), we had to shout be heard over the raging storm. The bride's family members would come one by one closer to the cot, distribute thalis (utensils) and shout out the name of the dish they were carrying, to serve. For getting served we had to raise the covering just enough to let them serve. The process would be repeated for second helping.

It was quite a while before the storm subsided and the mare I rode in on stubbornly stood still. It was quite a job to control her but I managed, despite being weighed down by my heavy attire and a silver crown.

After all that tamasha[9], the marriage was solemnized at midnight. It took a few more hours for the other ceremonies. It was a typical Punjabi wedding with two poetic renderings—the Sehra[10] and Bidai. Sehra is read when the marriage procession reaches the door of the bride's place. It is normally read by

---

[9]Commotion

[10]A poetic expression of all good things about the groom's family, praises for the bride and good wishes for the couple's bright future

Sehra

a close friend of the groom and when it is read loudly in poetic form, a joyous atmosphere descends over the landscape. All good things, true and imaginative in poetic form are said about the groom and people gleefully take out money to give to the reader. Whereas, the Bidai is normally read out by the family Pandit creating emotional and heart wrenching atmosphere as to what would be the scene when the bride leaves her house, leaving behind her own parents-brothers-sisters-friends. It made everybody cry, including me.

In those days, wedding celebrations lasted up to six or seven days at the bride's place. But my father was against such a burdensome affair, and we returned the next day. The return journey was in the same way, by changing buses, two trains and reaching Kaithal the next day.

As was customary in those days, the brother of the bride accompanied us, and returned with the bride after staying at our place for 4-5 days. After all the rituals ended: the bride going back to her parents' place, and my bringing her back, then visiting some close relatives, and so on, we went for our honeymoon, to Nainital, for a week. My in-laws had an establishment at Kichha in that district. We left Delhi by bus, first to Moradabad, then to Rampur and Rudarpur, and finally, to Kichha. We stayed in Kichha for one night and left the next day to see the resplendent Nainital hills.

MY PARENTS-IN-LAW, MY PRIDE

I dedicate this chapter to my parents-in-law. I feel fortunate to have been married into this family with its values; it is a matter of pride to write about them.

My father-in-law, Choudhary Ram Papneja, was born in 1920 in Pakistan. As the first child of the family, his mother desired for him to become the head of a village, a choudhary, and he was named Choudhary Ram. At the age of thirteen, he lost his father and all household responsibilities fell upon his young shoulders. Circumstances demanded he work as he had four siblings to look after: two brothers and two sisters, the youngest only six months old.

In 1946, he exchanged his father's property in Pakistan with a Muslim man who owned fields of red chillies and cotton, as well as orchards of oranges, maltas and other fruits, and a house in the village, just a year before the Partition. He was criticized vehemently by his elders; at the time, no one believed that the country would be divided. Later, the same people approached him when they needed shelter and work and he helped form the entire village. He aided those who had left for Pakistan and brought them back, even in the face of danger to his own life. He was brave, daring, helpful, disciplined and a born leader. Wherever he would pass by, people looked at him with reverence.

Over a period of time, he decided to shift to the Terai region of the Himalayas, where more fertile land was available at an economical price. Even before the wedding, my parents-in-law had moved away from the border village in Rajasthan to Nainital. It took a lot of courage for farmers to move to the Terai jungles inhabited by wild animals.

My parents-in-law acquired a good land holding and they had constructed a mud hut. Krishna, my wife, later narrated to me about how, when she was just barely thirteen, she would stay with her mother and younger brother in the mud hut. Many a night, while they were sleeping inside, a tiger would prowl around and eventually go to sleep on the other side of the wall. They could hear the animal's deep breaths.

Eventually, my father-in-law, with the help of a professional hunter, constructed a machan, and baited the tiger with a small goat. When the tiger finally appeared, my father-in-law shot the tiger inside the compound of their house.

At the time of my wedding, he was the sarpanch of Chak 50 GG of Rajasthan, and also the sarpanch of the surrounding villages around his farm in Terai, now in the state of Uttarakhand. He had lived to fulfil his mother's desire and more.

He was the first zila adhyaksh, the district head of the Bharatiya Jana Sangh in Nainital District. In those days, the future Prime Minister, Mr Atal Bihari Vajpayee, was the rashtriya adhyaksh, the national head of the Bharatiya Jana Sangh. They were on good terms. In 1971, my father-in-law stood for the elections as an MLA, against Narain Dutt Tiwari, a renowned Congress leader in UP. It was a tough fight watched by the entire nation. Although N.D. Tiwari was such a powerful opponent, he could only win by a slender margin of 127 votes.

Atal Bihari Vajpayee with my father-in-law

At the time of my wedding, my father-in-law and all his brothers lived together. They were a living example for the world: espousing real brotherhood, relationships, mutual respect and family values. His younger brothers looked up to him with awe, as if he were the Lord Ram himself. He always had the last word in family matters. I even noted how my father-in-law, on his part, took greater care of his brothers and their children. I often felt that this was unfair to his own children, as they did not get enough attention, but that was how my father-in-law was—taking pride always in being self-sacrificing.

I also must mention that though he was both a Rashtriya Swayam Sevak and Jana Sangh member, he was not against anybody based on religion, and only against those who spoke against the country. I have witnessed, with my own eyes, his love and affection for Muslims and other minorities.

My mother-in-law, Shrimati Kaushalya Rani provided a great deal of support to my father-in-law and always stood by him through thick and thin. She was a great lady, full of compassion and love. I bow my head in respect to her memory.

At times, destiny is cruel, even to people who least deserve it. My parents-in-law suffered greatly on account of the untimely deaths of their three eldest children: two sons and one daughter (my own wife, Krishna). It is difficult and almost unbelievable to imagine how, despite all those personal tragedies, they maintained their dignity and grace. One always felt humbled in the presence of their towering personalities.

I feel indebted to my in-laws for the values they imparted to my wife, especially her strength. Krishna was a pillar of strength to me—a direct reflection of their personalities.

I hold dear to me, Sudesh Chawla, my sister-in-law, Vijay Kumar Papneja, my brother-in-law and Sharda Arora, my younger sister-in-law. Sharda's son, Kushal Arora is working with us, and is a right hand to my son, Sanjay. Sharda's other two children, Shilpa and Kusha, are quite close to my children, as is Kushal's wife, Richa.

8

THE JOYS OF FAMILY LIFE

My eldest child, Sujata, was born on 7 July 1963. Sarita was born on 29 March 1965 and Savita on 20 September 1966 after which we had no intention of having any more children. However, my eldest sister, Lajwanti Goomber (who was more like a mother to us) ultimately prevailed upon my wife to persuade me to try and conceive a son.

What if we had another daughter, we asked her? She immediately assured us that she would look after the daughter herself! She advised us to visit a saint near Jalandhar for his blessings and took us there herself.

S.P. Rawal, Sujata, Krishna Rawal, PL Rawal, Sanjay, Ram Piari Rawal, Savita and Sarita, December 1974

In due course, we became the parents of a fourth child, our son, Sanjay. Sanjay was born on 19 October 1970, and our family was complete. Sanjay and my three daughters were born into a joint family: all my brothers and their families stayed together in Rana Pratap Bagh, Delhi. All of us were close.

I was as fond of telling stories to my children as to the children of my brothers. I crafted narratives out of thin air at their bequest: stories of the sea, mountains, jungles, caves, animals, trains and so on. I even created an imaginary character, Pip-Pip, who became the hero of all the stories. I made sure that each story had a happy ending, and I would always introduce monkeys, my children's favourite animal, in the story to make them laugh.

I have done the same for my grandchildren.

Sanjay as a toddler, posing with a Buddha statue larger than him

But a while before Sanjay's birth, I had a health scare. In 1967, sometime around June or July, blood suddenly began to gush out of my mouth; I was eventually diagnosed with tuberculosis. After extensive tests, the doctors decided to operate and remove one lobe from my right lung. Thus, I underwent a lobectomy operation at Tirath Ram Shah Hospital, Delhi in the month of August, 1967.

In a strange twist of fate, the operation failed. A clot formed and I went into a coma. Five senior doctors from all over Delhi were called on to discuss what could be done. After a long and serious hiatus, it was decided that I should be operated upon again in order to remove the clot. Failing this, the situation would be fatal for me.

This was not an easy decision for my family, but the doctors insisted we take the risk. My wife fainted in the hospital when she heard of the dire situation and had to be sent home.

My mother, on the other hand, displayed tremendous courage and stood at the door of the operation theatre and kept repeating:

> सतपाल ऐ ऑपरेशन तेरा नहीं है, मेरा है। जो कुछ भी होवेगा मैनू होवेगा, तू बिल्कुल ठीक हो जावेंगा।

> Satpal, this operation is not yours, but mine. If something goes wrong, it will happen to me, and you will be completely all right.

I am still impressed by the courage shown by my parents, my wife and my brothers, who stood vigil for me around the clock.

With the grace of God, the operation was successful and I recovered quickly. I was released from the hospital within fifteen days.

As the doctor advised me to stop driving my scooter

my relieved father bought me a second-hand car—a 1960 model Fiat—the keys to which he handed over as soon as I returned from the hospital. He also presented me with a new Seiko watch, which I have carefully preserved as part of my memorabilia.

9

A TRYST WITH DESTINY!

They say that 10% of life is what happens to you, and the remaining 90% is how you react to it. Man cannot discover new oceans and lands unless he gathers up the courage to lose sight of familiar shores.

The third incident that changed my life was nothing but a stroke of destiny.

I was working as a cashier in the LIC, but I was young and very restless; I wanted to switch jobs and take risks. I was an extrovert and quite close to everybody in the office, including almost all of my senior colleagues. On a fateful day—9th April 1964—a development officer, Swami, came up to me. He called for me and spoke to me in a disdainful and humorous tone, saying, 'What the heck are you doing, just sitting here wasting your time?' He then went on to tell me that he could get me a job with a UK-based company immediately, and that I should come with him. Right away.

Around 3 p.m., I closed the cash box, put the key in my

pocket and walked out of the office with Swami, without even seeking permission from my seniors. I had treated his offer like a joke. The LIC office was on the third floor of The Hindustan Times Building at Connaught Place. We exited the building and walked up to Scindia House, which was right around the corner. We came to a halt in front of an exclusive red-coloured elevator, and in all seriousness, Swami told me that I should get in that elevator and go up and visit the office of a company called Gestetner.

By this time, my patience was wearing thin. I spoke up, 'Come on, man! Tell me what this job is and who I must see. Why will he give me this job? Moreover, I am not even dressed properly for an interview!'

I was wearing a half-sleeved white shirt, paired with black trousers and black loafers (in what I thought of as the Raj Kapoor style, from the film *Awara*). In addition, I wore no socks, and had no tie. Swami ignored all this. He took off his tie and handed it over to me without a word.

He told me that I should ask to meet Cantem, who was the Regional Chief of the company, and to ask for the job of a salesman. Swami warned me not to speak to anyone else, only to Cantem. When I asked Swami what business the company was in, he replied saying that he had no idea at all.

I hesitated a little, but since I had nothing to lose, I knotted the tie around my neck and went up the elevator. The moment I opened the door and entered the premises, I saw a gentleman (whose name I later learned was Mohan Singh). On asking about Cantem, Mohan Singh began twirling his moustache, and wanted to know why I wanted to meet him. He began to question me. But I was in a carefree mood and retorted with a question, 'Are you Mr. Cantem?'. Of course, he replied in the negative.

This is where luck played its part: Cantem was sitting in the room and he heard us talking. He called for Mohan Singh to ask him what was happening. Mohan Singh told Cantem that someone had come for a job. Cantem ordered that I be sent in. So I knocked at the door, opened it and said, 'May I come in, Sir?'

Upon being asked to enter, I greeted him by name and stood 'at-ease' like I used to do in the NCC. Cantem stared at me over his half-moon spectacles. He looked me over, top to toe, remaining silent while he regarded me. He finally asked who I was and why I had come there.

I stated my name and said that I had come for a sales job. He again looked at me; he asked why he should select me when he had already received so many applications for the job.[11] He said this while opening his drawer to reveal a large stock of applications. I wasn't aware of anything at the time: I had no idea what the company sold or did. I was unused to expressing myself in English, but I was enthusiastic.

I still can't fathom why I said what I did. My simple straightforward honest reply was, 'Sir, I am handsome, I am smart and I can sell anything.'

At this he smiled and said, 'Okay, then sell me this pen.'

He picked up his green Parker pen and placed it in front of me. It had a gold cap. I was still standing at ease as he

---

[11] At the time, Gestetner was a 100% British Company, and people applied for jobs there with all kinds of recommendations. Youngsters from royal families and even bureaucrats were keen on joining the company.

had not asked me to sit down. I reached out and picked up the pen and slowly took off the cap. I put it back on a few times. I was stalling for time, thinking of the right words to say. Then, I turned around with the pen in my hand, and walked out of the room, closing the door behind me.

With flair, I opened the door, and asked again, 'May I come in, Sir?' He enthusiastically replied in the affirmative. 'Good afternoon to you, Mr. Cantem,' I began. 'My name is S. P. Rawal and I have come from the world's most famous pen company, Parker. This is a brand-new pen, the very latest model, and I would request that you write with it and feel its smooth form.' I handed over the pen and watched as he started scribbling on a piece of a paper. I continued, 'Mr Cantem, you are holding one of the finest pens in the world in your hand. Should it at any time give you any problem, we are here.' Cantem immediately looked up at me. 'Yup – that is Gestetner,' he said. The interview was over. He asked me to sit down and told me that I had gotten the job. He called for Mohan Singh again and asked him to get us two cups of coffee.

As we waited for the coffee to arrive, Cantem filled out a yellow form with my personal details. He spoke about himself and his story; he told me how he had joined as a junior technician and had risen to this position. I too could achieve that, he said as he pointed to his own chair. I could sit in there one day. He said that all they were looking for in a candidate was an ability to work hard with sincerity and honesty.

He asked me for my job application, and I had to tell him that I had not brought one. He found it funny that I had come for a job interview without an application. He inquired how I had found the office and who had told me about this job. This was tricky, as Swami had categorically told me not to mention his name, and had even said that if I did, I would be rejected. Having gotten the job, I did not want to make a misstep.

God must have been watching over me. I instantly responded that I had been having coffee at the Coffee House at lunch, and I overheard a few people talking. I had heard them mention a vacancy in the company. Curiously, Cantem asked who those people were and what they looked like. That was another tricky question, but I replied in a matter-of-fact way that there had been four people and that one of them was fat, handsome and looked like an Englishman. Cantem began to laugh and said that it must have been Sehgal. As I had nothing to say to this, I just kept quiet. Cantem then explained that the reason he was asking was that just a few minutes before I had walked in, a young man called Swami had been interviewed. He had told Swami that he was too smart for the job. I reflected that Swami was indeed very smart; he had a bachelors in English from St. Stephens College and could often be rather pushy. Cantem *had* mentioned that he did not like smart and pretentious applicants.

Well, my appointment letter was typed and Cantem said I should bring an application the next day. I was to write today's date on it and report to the branch office on Asaf Ali Road, where he would receive me at 9 a.m.—sharp. He also said that I was being appointed, but this was subject to clearing training and tests, which would take place in Calcutta sometime soon. Only after this would I be offered a formal letter of appointment.

Much later, Cantem admitted that his scrutiny when I entered his office had formed his first impression. He had, in that glance, made up his mind that I was the right person for the job.

When I came down from Mr. Cantem's office, I found Swami waiting for me near the elevator. Before I could say anything, he smirked. 'Rejected?', he asked. To his utter surprise, I held up my appointment letter. The look on his face was a sight for Gods to behold. The moral of the story: destiny can completely change the course of one's life. It changed mine, taking me from the cashier's table to a prime marketing job and enabling me to laugh at the man who had wanted to make a fool of *me*.

That day, when I returned home with the appointment letter from Gestetner, I was beside myself with excitement. I had joined a UK-based company. It was a rare privilege in those days, especially for a boy from a village who could hardly speak English. I could not even pronounce my company's name for days. I felt like a celebrity. Once I told my family, relations and friends what had happened they were full of praises. My wife, especially, was elated.

The next morning, I reached the Asaf Ali Road office at 9 a.m.—sharp—and Cantem himself opened the door for me and introduced me to everybody. He left me in the charge of the Senior Branch Manager, K.K. Kapoor—one of the finest branch managers at Gestetner. I was given an initial sales/mechanical training at the branch, and then sent for final training and tests to Calcutta.

Gestetner's training module was tough, but interesting.

We learned in a classroom, and then went into the field. Fourteen trainees had been selected from all over the country, and every Saturday, we would be tested on what we had learnt that week. I remember that every week, approximately three people were found to be not up to the mark and were asked to leave. Finally, there were only four trainees selected. And of these four, I was the only one who survived—and thrived—in the company until I retired.

The General Manager at that time, Mr. Eric Jessop, came to the training class to welcome us. He talked to us and made a statement that remains engraved on my mind: 'Gentlemen, Gestetner is a unique company where, if you work for even a day, whether during training or in a job, you will never forget the experience throughout your life'. This held true for me.

The company had such a delightful ambience and was so motivating that it was a joy to work there. One could rise as high in the company as one wanted to, through hard work and diligence, and God was kind to me. My thirty-six-year career at Gestetner always provided a wonderful and rewarding experience.

In fact, I was so successful at Gestetner and I earned so well that a shareholder of the company asked the Chairman how it was possible for an ordinary graduate to earn almost as much as the Chairman himself. The Chairman only replied, 'We wish we had many more like S.P. Rawal to enable the company to flourish many times over.'

Before I proceed narrating about my time at Gestetner, I would like to share that I was also involved in a parallel career. It was a duty to my family. Whether it was while I was in LIC (for those five years) or in Gestetner (until I was transferred to Calcutta), I devoted all my spare time to the family business of selling neckties or helping my brothers in their factory and shop. Gestetner gave us the weekend off, and I would even take leaves for tours for the family business. I would sell neckties in Delhi or in cities like Jaipur, Jodhpur, Bareilly, Kanpur, Lucknow and even Patna and Calcutta. It was tough when I look back on this time, especially in the beginning. I would leave Delhi on the nightly train or on a bus with an attaché case full of ties, weighing around 30-40 kilograms, on my shoulder. I would arrive in the city, find a modest guest house or a dharamshala and start out. As I could not afford to hire help, I would carry the heavy attaché case on my shoulder and visit shop to shop to show, canvass and sell the ties. I was young, full of zeal and these difficulties did not matter to me. It was such fun to earn money for the family. As the business grew, I did start hiring a rickshaw for the whole day at the rate of rupees 5 per day.

THE JOB

11th May 1964. My first day on the job. It coincided with the date of my marriage anniversary. Unfortunately, it was also the same day that the first prime minister of the country, Jawaharlal Nehru, died on. I remember that I was still in the field when all the offices began to close and shope pulling down their shutters.

My starting salary was rupees 130 per month, plus incentives. However, within three years, my income grew exponentially.

Most of the salespeople at Gestetner were young men

from well-to-do backgrounds, and even royal families. I was exposed to their work culture during my first few days on the job. The workday of the sales force would theoretically begin at 9 a.m. when everyone first assembled at the office before moving out to make sales calls by 10 a.m. The target was to make ten or fifteen sales calls a day, in person, with a monthly sales target of business worth Rs 7,500. During one of these early days at work, I realized that I wanted to do things differently. Most of the sales force left the office and gathered at a restaurant called La Boheme for an hour of lazy conversations and coffee. They would set off at 11 a.m. to meet clients. Often, meeting clients was only a pretext for more loitering.

For a couple of days, I went along with them to La Boheme. Soon enough, I realized two things: first, this was not the kind of life I was used to and second, I wanted to prove to myself and to the world that I could rise to the occasion. I wanted to do my best, work hard and dedicate myself to the job.

Since Gestetner was a well-known company, clients wanted to meet with the salesmen first. My personal charisma, persuasiveness and persistence helped me persuade my clients. I strongly believed and worked with this mantra: Don't sell the product, sell yourself means get yourself accepted. I wanted the client to see me as the upright, knowledgeable and honest person. It is important to win over the client with integrity and commitment to gain his trust. Having done that, selling is easy. All that the client expects from you is dedication and service.

Though my initial sales target was a business of Rupees

7500/-per month, my personal target changed. I wanted to achieve the target by the 15th or, at the latest, the 20th of the month. This meant that I could start the next month at an advantage. This enthusiasm allowed me to achieve my targets every single month for many years. In the forty-eight months that I worked as Service Representative I never missed my target—a record by itself.

Learning as I worked, I began to establish record after sales record. My final record was a whopping 1235% of my target in four months, and against a target of 400%. This record was not broken by anyone during all my years at Gestetner.

I was promoted several times. I was the youngest Sales Supervisor at thirty, Assistant Manager at thirty-two, the youngest Branch Manager at thirty-four, the youngest Branch Manager of a Metropolitan Branch at thirty-six, the youngest Zonal Manager at forty-eight, and the youngest Vice President at fifty-seven. I finally retired at sixty, even though the retirement age then was fifty-eight. My first promotion to Sales Supervisor was to Calcutta Branch in the year 1970.

TURBULENT WEST BENGAL

In those days Calcutta was in turmoil. The Naxalite movement had erupted and the masses had risen up against the establishment. It was anarchy. I saw people snatching money and valuables and any belongings. If you were having dinner at a restaurant, there was a risk that a group of people would come and sit with you, forcefully dine with you, and ask you to pay. And you dared not ask any questions.

That the situation was serious was known all over the

country. The media reports splashed across the newspapers daily. My father and my family were terrified for me. My father even asked me to resign rather than move to Calcutta after my promotion. He declared that if I wanted the promotion and wanted to be a so-called Sahib, I would have to go alone without my family accompanying me. But I was so enthused and excited at the prospect of becoming a Manager that I wanted to grab this opportunity. I pleaded with everyone to let me go, and I finally managed to convince them.

At that time, it was decided that I would go to Calcutta alone, but would call the family on the telephone once a week and come home once a month, even if it was only for a day or two. And I did.

It will not be out of place to mention, with historic background, the overall scene in West Bengal during the Naxalite movement. It pained me to see the desperate lows of the natives. Almost every Bengali with an opportunity to leave their birthplace, did so gleefully. And in most cases, they never returned.

West Bengal once was the seat of knowledge, a hub of industrial activities, the capital of culture and a prolific producer of sportspersons in India. It was a vibrant place, but unfortunately, it all changed during those days. A number of foreign companies had their headquarters in Calcutta, and there are hundreds of sad stories of how the corporate world was forced to shift away from Calcutta. I mention herein only two instances:

1. Mr. Aditya Birla, the doyen of Indian industry, described by Manmohan Singh, the prime minister as 'among the best and brightest citizens of India'— India's first global industrialist was dragged out of his car between GPO and RBI, beaten and had his clothing torn. That very night, Mr. Birla left Calcutta for good and moved with his empire to Mumbai.
2. The company, Philips, left the land where it was born during this period. Their worldwide head had come to visit the Beliaghata factory. He was not allowed to enter the factory by the left union there. He waited for over an hour, even asked for help from the state administration but in vain. Within one night, the board decided to shift all their investments to other states, away from Calcutta.

People were afraid for their lives and the threat of brutal murder was everywhere. Ten to twelve murders in a day was considered a relatively peaceful one. I remember being witness to a terrible scene while I was walking along a terribly busy and popular market, Barra Bazaar, with the company's salesman. I saw a bus being driven at an extremely dangerous speed through the market, its horns blaring. The bus seemed to be empty except for the driver and another person. A human head that had been chopped off was tied to the front of the radiator. Blood dripped from it onto the street. It was horrifying. Another time, I opened the window of my room at the YMCA in Chowringhee, and I was greeted by the horrifying sight of a corpse floating in the pond.

COMMUNICATION

In 1970, telecom facilities were poor. You would have to wait for hours and days on end to get through to another person. Few could afford a telephone of their own. We did not have a phone in the house, but we used the one in our factory. Every Sunday, the whole family, dressed as if going to a festival, would assemble in the factory and wait for my call on the telephone.

I was in Calcutta and would go to the post office, book a call for 9 a.m. and wait for my turn. STD facilities were unavailable, so the call could take an hour or more to connect. Once the call went through, everybody would take turns to talk to me, and they would ask when I would be back in Delhi.

I was often moved to tears. Once, when everybody else had had their turn, Baby—as we fondly called Savita—approached the phone; she was four years old at the time. Everybody coaxed her, asking her to greet me. She folded her tiny hands in front of the mouthpiece of the telephone, and said, 'Namaste Bauji.' This little act touched me deeply.

Apart from the weekly telephone calls, I also received letters almost every day from some family member or the other. Each of these I read many times over, moved by the sincere, honest and touching emotions in them. I have preserved them like treasures. These are very emotional letters—from my respected father, and all the way to generations of children. One letter from my beloved mother consists of a large impression of her palm; she could not write and had someone add, on her behalf, her best wishes for my well-being. I have selected a few of the many letters for you to read at the end of this narrative.

As planned, I travelled to Delhi every month. I would board the Rajdhani Express on Friday evening from Calcutta, reach Delhi on Saturday at 10.30 a.m., spend time with my family, or visit my parents at Kaithal, and then board the train back to Calcutta on Sunday evening so as to be back in the office on Monday morning.

Every single time I visited home, I was pressured to resign as the situation in Calcutta kept worsening. I was in the midst of things and could not conceptualize the anxieties for those who were far away, with only access to the media. I went out, even at night, enjoying myself at a variety of restaurants in Park Street. Firpo's, Trinca's, Bluefox or Flury's. Those were interesting times.

FAMILY VALUES & BONDS

During one of my customary visits to Delhi, in March of 1971, I was surprised to see my father and my elder brother at the station, waiting to receive me. Of all the members of my family, my father rarely came to receive me all the way from Kaithal. But I soon learnt of the reason. My father handed a letter over to me and asked me to sign it. He asked me to take it immediately to my office and hand it over.

It was a letter of resignation. My father spoke. He said that although I may be enjoying my role of a supervisor, he could not ignore his fears about my safety. As his son, I should not question his decision. He said that he would take full responsibility for my rehabilitation.

I did not want to go against the wishes of my father, or my family. I left for the office and handed over the letter.

It was difficult to convince the senior managers: Mr. F.C. Lyons, the Managing Director, and Mr. D.N. Sarkar, the Financial Director. They personally spoke to me and said that I had a bright future ahead of me in Gestetner. They did not want me to take such a drastic step. But I had no choice and, ultimately, they had to agree.

After I had resigned, I stayed at home in Delhi, ruminating over my options: what business should I start? Should I be part of the family business? But I did not want to sit in the shop at Sadar Bazar, or go out selling neckties. I went to Kaithal and, after a lot of deliberation, it was decided that I should either start a rice mill or open a steel dealership. My father and my youngest brothers would help me manage the business. While we were still debating over these different options, an unfortunate incident occurred. My younger brother, dear Iqbal, who was looking after another family operation—a small sugar mill at Muzaffar Nagar—had a serious accident.

Iqbal was at the mill at night and a small piece of cane leaf flew into one of his eyes. He was already blind in one eye, but the debris took away his other eye as well. The local doctors were not sure that his eyesight would ever return.

The whole family was shaken. My father went to visit him and decided that I should be entrusted with the responsibility to help Iqbal. I was to not consider any other options until Iqbal's eyes were restored. I accepted this responsibility and I took my brother and his wife, Raj Rani, to the doctors.

It was a pity that such a robust and young man had to undergo such agony. It took us almost three months before we found the right ophthalmologist, Dr Hari Mohan, and Iqbal was on his way to recovery. Ultimately, it was Iqbal's willpower and desire to get better that brought his eyesight back. He got better day by day while undergoing natural treatment. I was happy I could be of help to him.

Six months had passed, and I was still without a job or responsibility. After Iqbal recovered, my father left it to me to decide what venture I wanted to start. He offered to help in whatever way he could.

But my concerns were mounting. I had begun to worry about my children's education. I was keen to send my children to better schools, maybe even a good boarding school, for their future successes. My father supported this, but he admitted that it would not be proper that my children study in private schools while my elder brothers send their children to government schools.

I knew he was right, but I felt depressed about the situation, worried that I was not doing anything constructive to improve my lifestyle. My wife supported me, saying that she would stand by whatever decision I took. She said that all she needed was the bare minimum and she would manage the household and look after the children.

As six months had passed, I went to the Gestetner office to collect my PF(Provident Fund).

Again, destiny reared its head.

I was waiting near the accounts department when Sarkar, the Financial Director, walked in and remarked that he was happy to see me. He asked after my affairs and was saddened to know that I hadn't started anything anew. He inquired whether I would like to join Gestetner—once again. I immediately said, 'Yes, if you take me back in the position from which I resigned.' He took me to his room and asked me to wait.

He went to inform Lyons who was equally happy to hear about me.

When I walked into his room, Lyons laughed and taunted me, 'See, I told you not to leave Gestetner, and you did so against my advice.' I replied that it had been due to circumstances, but that I was back now. He said.

Mr Watkin was the Marketing Manager now, and only he could decide and so, Lyons asked for him. Watkin came in and was briefed. He offered me, immediately, the job of Machine Salesman, and that too in New Delhi itself. I would report to Mr. Bahl who was my contemporary and a good friend. I politely declined as I wanted the same position I had when I left.

I didn't mind being posted anywhere, but I would join only as Supervisor. Watkin was asked to take me to his office to work out a solution and report back to Lyons. The message was loud and clear: I was to be accommodated. The result was that a job was created for me in Chandigarh. I accepted it.

When I returned home with this news my family was disappointed. My father felt that he had not done enough to help me, and that I had not given him enough time to come to a solution. However, my wife was happy for me.

CAREER AT GESTETNER

The rest, as they say, is history.

Once again, I joined Gestetner as the Machine Supervisor at Chandigarh in August 1971. I was in Chandigarh for four months, after which I was promoted and sent to Bombay (now Mumbai) as Assistant Manager-Machine in January 1972.

My old Manager at Calcutta, Ravi Mohan, had moved to the Bombay branch and had informed Lyons that he needed me at Bombay for the launch of a new model.

Life in Bombay

Outside the office in Bombay, we had many family outings. Almost every Sunday, Krishna, Sujata, Sarita, Savita, Sanjay and I would visit Juhu Beach, only a short distance from our house in Andheri (West). My younger sister, Suraksha, would accompany us with her husband, Hashmat Rai Guglani, and the children, Poonam, Kaley and Sanjay, as they lived nearby. Both the families would bring home-cooked food and reach Juhu Beach early in the morning. We would share the food. It often seemed like the whole beach belonged to us, as there were hardly any people there in those days, except for a few folk out on morning walks. The beaches were clean too. I remember Krishna would give Sanjay an oil massage, and Hashmat Rai and I would get massages there. It used to be such fun.

I remember a small (but significant) incident during my time in Bombay. As I was walking down the road one day, my pocket was picked. I had a large sum in my pocket, a thousand rupees. Frantic about the loss, I wrote a letter to my father informing him. Lo and behold, the very next week I got a money order for double the amount from my father, as well as a letter from my younger brother who was in Kaithal at the time. My younger brother wrote that I should not worry at all about the loss and that they were always there for me. Even though I was thirty-two-years old and had four kids *and* a good job, my parents were still worried and concerned about losses incurred by me or any of their children. However old I may be, I was still a child to my parents. I was touched. I feel this reflects the values of their generation and the love they had for me. Though it may sound a minor incident and a meagre amount, it reflects the strength of our bonds. When I look back on this, the sense of care, affection and an ever-ready desire to help one another through thick and thin becomes abundantly clear to me.

I remained in Bombay for a relatively short time. After twenty seven months, my team and I made record sales and, as a reward, I was promoted as Branch Manager and transferred to Roorkee in April 1974.

Golden Era of My Career

This was my first posting as an independent branch manager. Even though the Roorkee Branch was a small business center, by God's grace, I beat the sales records every month continuously for seven months while I was there. The business of the branch grew 500 per cent within this period.

The management was so happy with my performance that, deviating from normal convention, the Chairman and Managing Director of Gestetner in India, Frederick C. Lyons and the Financial Director, D.N. Sarkar (a later Chairman), visited the branch to celebrate and commend me.

A rare visit. The CMD, F.C. Lyons, at Roorkee in 1974

Consequently after their visit, I was promoted as Deputy Manager of the Delhi Branch, one of the biggest branches in the country. Within two years of my appointment, the Delhi branch too made records. I was promoted to full Manager of the Delhi branch in 1976-77. By August 1979, the Delhi branch was the first branch in the history of Gestetner to cross a crore of business sales. The Delhi branch created history, by growing from 36 lakh to ONE CRORE a year. There was great jubilation and celebration, and every member of the branch was rewarded amply.

Again, destiny had different plans.

One day, the chairman called me to his office and commended me on leading the branch so brilliantly. He said the company needed my services at Chennai, a branch that had great potential but had not been performing up to their expectations. He felt that only I could take the Chennai branch to the position it deserved. It was the biggest challenge in my career—I had to convert a loss-making area to a profit centre. Thus, I was transferred to Chennai in October 1979 as a branch manager of two combined branches, Madras (now Chennai) and Coimbatore.

Everybody in the family was upset by the news of this move. It would affect the children's education midway. Chennai was so far away, they said. However, the transfer turned out to be a blessing in disguise. It was the best thing that could have happened to me: in terms of my career, my family, my children, and my social status.

When I took charge of Chennai + Coimbatore branches they were making three lakhs a month. With God's grace, within three years, the branch averaged thirty lakhs per month. And thus, I was promoted as the Zonal Manager of the South Zone in 1981; the youngest zonal manager in the history of Gestetner.

Life in Chennai was eventful and satisfying. My children's education and our social circle flourished there. I can say that the best years of my working life were spent there. The southern zone I was in charge of was soon contributing 75% of the total profit made by the company. As such, I was much sought after and was well-received by one and all, in India as well as in England. My wife and I often remarked, while in Chennai, that we wanted 'time to stop here'.

Along with all the good things happening sometimes one faces health issues which take enormous proportion in the later years. In 1981 I was diagnosed with Menniers syndrome in my right ear resulting in making me deaf in this ear. And even this process took about 8-9 years, in which time I was subjected to fits and vomiting. It was tough managing on the job but with God's grace I could sail through.

Socially, my circle had expanded, especially due to Panna Lalji Tatia, one of the finest person I've met in the course of my life, and his family; they became part of my family. He was a well-connected man in all circles of Chennai. I joined the Madras Gymkhana Club within a week's time after application, courtesy Late F.V. Arul, former director of CBI.

To top it off, I was very proud of my children, who were excelling in their studies. Sujata had been admitted to an excellent engineering college, Sarita had begun to study dentistry and the baby of the house, Savita, was on her way to becoming a doctor and was pursuing her MBBS at Kilpauk Medical College. Sanjay, brilliant as he was, had handled the shift from Don Bosco School to DAV school well. It was one of the prime schools in South India, and it followed the CBSE syllabus.

I was enjoying every moment of life, and what a life that was! I was on top of the world! We lived in our happy world; the family attachments growing stronger by the day. Routinely, every Sunday, the family would drive down to VGP beach at 7 a.m., which was surprisingly empty. We would run around in the sand and play games, enjoying those precious moments. On the way back home, we would stop at a small restaurant where the staff had started looking forward to our Sunday visits. They would serve us an exclusive family-sized 4-feet-long dosa. We'd sit on two opposite sides of the table and eat to our heart's content.

But family came first, and it began to prove difficult to connect to our relatives and even locate a groom for our eldest daughter. Eventually, and after my persistent requests, the management at Gestetner agreed to my transfer. I moved back to Delhi in October 1988, after I had completed nine golden years at Chennai.

Achievement and Reward

My career at Gestetner spanned over three decades, during which I was fortunate enough to work with many unique leaders. I must mention two of them, Denis Lowry and Paul Wilkinson. They were incredible personalities and motivated me profoundly.

Mr Denis Lowry

In 1969, early during my career at Gestetner, a scheme called 'Aage Badho' (Move Forward) was floated by Denis Lowry, over four months, during which the target was to achieve at least 400 per cent of the usual sales target. By the end of those four months, I topped the list with a 1245 per cent. Lowry was so impressed with me that he invited me to his office in Scindia House, where I had been interviewed so many years ago. Inviting all the staff at the office, he opened a bottle of champagne to celebrate my achievement. I was also presented with the key to a Chevrolet Impala; he said that the car and the chauffeur were waiting for me downstairs. I could use it to go wherever I wished to for a week, all on the company account. I was also asked to take a holiday with my wife, go anywhere in the country, on the company account.

I was elated with the car. I wanted to drive it everywhere. We went straight to my house in Rana Pratap Bagh, sitting in the backseat of the car; when it was parked in front of our house my family could hardly believe their eyes. They were all so proud of me. The next morning, Krishna and I drove the Impala to Kaithal to meet my parents. When we arrived at Kaithal, the car was too wide to enter the gate to the village. We had to leave the car outside the town, parked in front of the Municipal Corporation's office. We then took a rickshaw to my parents' house.

We left the house as soon as we arrived, since my parents' happiness knew no bounds. We decided to go where the car was parked, taking two rickshaws back to the municipal office. My parents took the time to dress formally for the celebration. My wife and my mother sat on one rikshaw and on the other me and my father. Word had already spread, like fire across the small town, and people passing our rickshaw extended their greetings to my father. He responded with such great pride. Finally, we arrived at the spot which was surrounded by a curious crowd.

Accepting greetings and congratulations, we climbed into the car and drove to a family agricultural land, a few kilometres away. What a proud ride it was for my parents; when we reached the field, the workers assembled to receive all of us and the car, and celebrated with dance and song.

After returning to Delhi, we also drove to the Taj Mahal in the car, with a few other colleagues who had participated in Lowry's scheme. It was a memorable visit.

As far as the second offer to travel, my wife and I went to Srinagar and stayed at the Hotel Oberoi Palace, an erstwhile Maharaja's palace that had been converted into a hotel. My elder brother and sister-in-law also joined us (at their own cost) to spend time with us. The seven days we spent in Kashmir were indeed heavenly.

We dined at the Oberoi Palace, and on one occasion, the banquet manager extended his courtesies to us specifically. I distinctly remember drinks at the bar, called 'Under the Banyan Tree', which overlooked the mesmerizing Dal Lake. After drinks, when my wife and I entered the dining hall, we were served lavishly. A waiter recommended that I try their sherry, and I agreed. I was so excited that I downed sixteen pegs of sherry and yet remained sober that evening. The film stars, Rajesh Khanna and Asha Parekh and the whole team were also at the Oberoi, shooting their upcoming film, *Aan Milo Sajna*. We had tea together and Rajesh Khanna himself invited us to watch the shooting at Char Chinar. The shooting was slated to take place at night and my brother expressed his desire to accompany us. We journeyed there in a shikara over the Dal Lake in the dark of night. It was quite scary as it was a moonless night, but we greatly enjoyed ourselves.

After returning to Delhi, I was again summoned by Lowry and given an official award. The whole experience: winning the sales competition, the car, the trip, and the rewards that followed made me feel a sense of immense accomplishment.

But this success had its share of anxiety. Out of the 1245 per cent sales target I had overachieved, I had received an order worth almost 300 per cent from a single customer—The National Institute of Family Planning (NIFP)[12], and this was the largest order ever received by the company then. However, there was a catch. The order was not completely official; it had been sent for approval to the Ministry of Health, Government of India (GOI). The client had placed the order in my order book after going through all the formalities, but had said that a formal sanction would have to be taken from the ministry. While I had calculated this order, the approval was yet to come.

While enjoying the champagne and the celebrations, I received a call stating that the Ministry had raised a few queries about the order and had instructed that the orders be kept in abeyance. I felt as if the ground was slipping away from beneath my feet.

But I did not show any signs of this impending disaster, and after the celebrations were over, I quietly left. The only person I took into confidence was my wife.

But every day that followed, I was in despair and agony. I kept trying to have the order regularised. I decided to meet

---

[12]Now called the National Family Planning Institute

the director himself on whose sanction the order was placed. Over a period of time, I had developed a good rapport with him. Unfortunately, I was told he was hospitalized. My wife and I, both visited the hospital with flowers—a courtesy call. Luckily, we found that he had recovered and would be back home the next day.

The Director joined the office after a week, I met him and apprised him of the whole story. I informed him that just in case, for whatever reason, the order does not get approved, I would like to resign from my job and showed him the resignation letter which I was carrying with me (in fact I handed over the letter to him to post to my office in case the order does not go through, but he said to keep it with me and that it would not be required). He was genuinely moved and took it as a challenge as his own prestige was involved too as he had sanctioned the order. He assured me not to worry, give him a week to ten days and he would ensure that the order was regularized. He said the order was placed as per their requirements and that they had the money. Only an approval was required from the ministry and he would get that.

Eventually, and by God's grace, the order was finally regularized, but it took roughly a month—a period so full of anxiety I could almost feel the sword hanging over my head. But as they say: all's well that ends well.

Mr Paul Wilkinson

Paul Wilkinson was the second person in Gestetner to influence me immensely. He was a great trainer and motivator. He started the in-house training program called STS ('Success through Sales'). He believed in the dictum, 'Give me a man with burning desire, and I will produce a winner'. He hated letting potential colleagues go, and instead preferred to train them better. He firmly believed that those who were not doing well only needed further training.

In Gestetner, many people were asked to be in charge of training sessions and for two years, I was also given the additional charge for training as the Principal of STS when I was the General Manager of the Northern Zone. Teaching was a learning experience for me.

I distinctly remember an instance regarding Wilkinson. He had a driver by the name of Thakur, and one day, he discovered that the man was an alcoholic. Worse, in one of the office parties where Wilkinson was present he became totally drunk and misbehaved. Under normal circumstances, the driver would have been sacked or at least removed from MD's duty. However, Wilkinson being Wilkinson, instead of getting rid of the driver counselled the man and helped him until he was reformed and no longer an alcoholic.

There was another incident where a young sales executive had been asked by his reporting manager to leave the organization due to non-performance. When Wilkinson came to know of the case, he set up a meeting with the executive and asked him to generate just five business prospects daily without worrying about the target. The man was put under the guidance of a senior person. After three months the same executive not only achieved his targets but qualified for the prize scheme. Wilkinson held the belief that everyone has the potential, one only needed to know how to help them achieve it.

Mr Wilkinson had a knack of floating competitive schemes, and would handsomely reward the winners. One of his unique schemes had both, a very tough target and a very attractive prize—an incredible car. In 1997, under that scheme, I topped the sales in a specific product—our digital copy printer and was declared a winner of the brand-new luxury car, a Maruti EsteemVX. I was brimming with pride when I went in to celebrate with Wilkinson and my other colleagues at their office. This was the first time in the history of Gestetner that anybody had received a premier car as an award, and I was the first one to receive it.

Soon after, Wilkinson went back to England, like he did every year for Christmas. One day he called from London to ask whether I had already received the car during the festive period. He insisted that I buy the car within the next three days and receive him from the airport in the brand-new car upon his return to India.

This proved to be a challenge for our finance department, as the Maruti Esteem VX was not in stock. But the showroom arranged for it when they heard of the situation. I had called my son, Sanjay, to join me while taking the delivery of the car, and I remember how proud I felt when Sanjay drove the new car home.

By 1997 Gestetner had become part of Ricoh and were selling their products. There was an invitation from Ricoh to visit their factory. As part of his motivational traits Wilkinson deputed me along withK.B Menon to visit the Ricoh factory, Tohoku, Japan. It was such an honour. When we reached the factory the Indian national tricolour flag was flying along with the Japanese national flag, atop the factory. Great feeling. In the factory I was asked to speak about India and its culture in front of all the Japanese workers assembled in a hall. On the dais were senior executives of Ricoh. It was an experience of a lifetime, to speak with the help of an interpreter. The only time in my life. In the evening the host took us to Hill Resort near Tohoku, which was considered to be the best in that region. What an experience—to sit, the next morning, in the hot water jacuzzi along with Japanese men and women, overlooking snow-peaked mountains. It was WOW.

After the Japan visit I had planned to visit the USA for the first time to meet my daughters. April 13 1997, it was such a thrilling experience, while flying from Tokyo to San Francisco, to see live on TV in the plane —Tiger Wood winning the prestigious Master Tournament—his first GREEN COAT at the age of 21 by a record 12 strokes in Augusta. He was the youngest player to win this. Also, this was the first time I was using a mobile phone to speak to my daughter from the plane.

Mr Wilkinson's charisma, innovative thought process, meritorious schemes and encouraging attitude helped create a winning team under his leadership. Thank you, Wilkinson for giving me these experiences of a lifetime.

In 1998, I was promoted to the post of Vice-President of Gestetner and remained so till my retirement in October 2000.

Gestetner

29.9.2000

ORGANISATIONAL ANNOUNCEMENT

Mr. S P Rawal, Vice President (Special Projects) is retiring w.e.f. 30th September 2000 after 37 years of glorious service with Gestetner. Mr. Rawal joined this company in the year 1964 as Service Representative and worked his way up to the position of Vice President.

During the span of 37 years he became synonymous with success. To his credit he has a plethora of records which still remain unsurpassed such as not missing his budget even once in 48 months as Service Representative. Based on his splendid and consistent performance he was promoted in 1981 as the youngest ever Zonal Manager.

Mr. Rawal is the first person in the history of Gestetner India Ltd. who was rewarded an "Esteem VX" car by the company in February, 96 for his achievements in business.

His career graph commensurate with his brilliant and consistent performance steadily rose and from the position of General Manager he became VP (Sales) in April 1998. His product knowledge coupled with his phenomenal demonstration skills has made him a leader par excellence and a constant source of inspiration to others. He is a classical good soldier who led from the front.

We wish him a happy retired life.

K Swetharanyan
Managing Director

10

MY CHILDREN

While my career flourished, my children were also fulfilling our dreams. In 1980 while we were still in Chennai, Sujata had achieved distinction and qualified for both medicine and engineering. I received the news that she had gotten into a medical college while I was in an official meeting in the headquarters at New Delhi. I remember distributing sweets to everybody and feeling extremely proud. My first child had taken the lead. When I returned to Chennai, all my family members had come to receive me at the airport. As we sat in the car, my wife quietly whispered that Sujata had got a letter for admission to an engineering college as well. I instantly insisted that she take up medicine only.

Very few women in those days opted to go in for engineering, and I was worried for her. For a few days, I was adamant that Sujata pursue a career in medicine and the atmosphere in the house soured. Sujata tried her best to convince me, reminding me about my father's words: 'one can only excel in what he or she likes to do'. Finally, I relented when she said, 'Bauji, I don't like blood or surgeries; chances are that I might leave medicine halfway through, which you would not like.' On hearing this I understood her, and I began to cry. I embraced her, expressing my regret that she had to take on such stress because of my adamant attitude and told her to go ahead and do what she wanted. She responded splendidly by doing extremely well for herself. She managed to get a scholarship on her own to pursue higher education in the USA and went there to do her MS, and later her PhD too.

Sarita, my second daughter, had done equally well. She joined a Dental College at Annamalai University, Chidambaram, and later for internship, Madras Dental College in Chennai. Sarita has always been the boldest of the daughters and she took equally well to other activities like drama, declamation, hosting shows, as well as art, especially painting. She is also responsible and most of the decisions in the family are taken with her input.

Savita, who I always think of as Baby, did equally well. She got admission, on her own merit, in Government Kilpauk Medical College, Chennai to pursue her MBBS degree. She did her internship at Safdarjung Hospital, and her MS (Ophthalmology) from Medical College, Rohtak. She finally completed her fellowship from LV Prasad Institute, Hyderabad, which is a rare feat for an ophthalmologist.

Sanjay, my son, has always been an all-rounder: good at table tennis, chess and rowing, while excelling academically. He was such a smart youngster that he received the second-highest grade for economics during his CBSE exams.

Despite enjoying ourselves in Chennai, we shifted back to Delhi by the time my daughters were all grown up: Sujata was twenty-five and in the USA; Sarita at twenty-four had finished her BDS, and was doing her residency at Safdarjung Hospital, and Savita was finishing her MBBS course and would start her internship in Delhi. My wife and I began to search for suitable grooms for my children, but it was difficult while we were based in Chennai. Sanjay too had joined B.Com (Hons.) in Sri Ram College of Commerce (SRCC) in Delhi. On my specific requests, I was transferred to Delhi as Zonal Manager in October 1988.

Luckily, while I was in Chennai, I had applied for a three-bedroom flat in a DDA scheme. I was incredibly lucky to get a three-side-open flat in Hauz Khas, New Delhi, by draw of lots. Owning a house is a dream for everyone; getting one in posh South Delhi was just icing on the cake.

11

A DARK PHASE

As soon as we settled down in Delhi, we started meeting people to find a prospective groom for our eldest daughter. Everything seemed to be going well, but tragedy struck us soon.

On 17 February 1990, my wife was on her way to meet her father, along with her younger sister and her children in a car. The car was driven by a chauffeur and met with an accident, colliding with a bus on the highway near Hapur, about 90 kilometres from Delhi. It was a head-on collision. The chauffeur died instantly, and my wife suffered a severe head injury and began bleeding profusely. My sister-in-law and her children were also injured.

A traveller brought my wife to the nearest hospital at Hapur where the doctors declared her 'brought dead'. I am told she could have survived had immediate medical help been provided, but alas, that did not happen.

My life changed, and it changed forever. Grief overcame

all of us, including the children. And I now had too many responsibilities to manage all by myself: the household, my demanding job, along with the responsibility of helping my grown children settle in their jobs and with their families. It required a lot of sustained effort.

It was luck that our domestic help, Lil Bahadur, who had been with us since a young age took complete charge of the house. He was a godsend. Right from buying vegetables, to cooking, to maintaining the house and even attending to visitors was done by him during such a difficult time. Every single person who came to the house had only praise for him. I will always remember him for his support.

My parents-in-law also provided me with much support. My mother-in-law stayed with us after the tragedy and helped us all cope. Sujata, too, came back from the USA after her mother's death and stayed back for my sake. But in my heart of hearts, I knew this was not where she wanted to be.

They say that trouble never comes alone. During this period I had suffered heavy financial losses forcing me to sell the flat and shift to a smaller house. With God's grace I reinvented myself, worked hard on the job, was promoted from GM to VP and life came back on track . At the same time Sanjay started excelling in his profession thus bringing back the glory of the house.

My Luck, My Wife: Krishna

I enjoyed twenty-nine wonderful years with my wife. Rarely ever had we argued, and we had shared understanding, wholehearted support, absolute commitment, complete devotion and utmost care. Krishna deserves all credit for raising our wonderful children and for encouraging and motivating them to achieve; I had always been busy building my career that I devoted too little time to the family. But she did more than I ever could have, single-handedly.

Her passing away has been my biggest setback. She was, and still is, my good luck charm. I could endlessly list her qualities, but I will only share a few here:

1. Live within one's own limit. Whatever be your level you can live contended -it's possible. Having more (money-materialist things) does not ensure Happiness—it's you and only you which decide how much you wish to be happy.
2. Personally she would be happier sacrificing than gaining.
3. Never ever Give up—there is surely going to be a better tomorrow.
4. Never ever say bad things about others—Don't indulge in gossips. She was one unique lady who would never indulge/enjoy gossips.
5. Keep up your Self Esteem even in adverse circumstances. If you decide to do so you will find your way without disturbing the equilibrium of the house. It is not easy but she was a very self disciplined/determined/forthright lady.

From the records kept by our family pandit at Haridwar. He has records spanning seven generations.

My brother-in-law, Vijay Papneja, the younger brother of my wife, has also narrated the events of that fateful day below.

- God has bestowed me with enough: the best things and the best relations. When I recall my elder sister, Krishna Rawal, I am reminded of a childhood spent beside her. I was fortunate to learn the values I have from her, as she was one of the greatest souls on earth.
- 17th February, 1990 is a day I will never forget. My elder sister passed away while travelling from Delhi to Kiccha in Uttarakhand. She had come to visit and to inquire about the well-being of our father who had been quite ill. She, along with another of my sisters,. Sudesh Chawla and her daughters, Neha and Payal, were on the way to Kiccha in their car.
- When they reached Garh Ganga, Brijghat-Hapur in Ghaziabad, the driver tried to overtake a bus. Unnoticed by them, a bus was speeding from the opposite direction. A deadly collision ensued. Krishna di, Sudesh di and her daughters were sitting in the backseat. Krishna di had anticipated a crash, and had hurriedly pushed Neha off her lap to the left. She herself remained in the line of the danger on the right side.
- The collision was terrible. The right side of her body was completely injured in the accident. However, she did not lose consciousness and reaching out with her left arm, she checked whether Neha was safe and sound. Her concern for others was so great that she never thought of herself. Had she not pushed Neha

away in time, the little girl would have suffered life-threatening injuries. On the way to the hospital, she breathed her last.

- It was the worst day of my life; I lost my ideal, my sister, on that unfortunate day. But I have always been proud and fortunate to be her younger brother, and still am. Her greatness is still remembered by all.

12

MY DIAMONDS, MY PEARLS, MY JEWELS AND MY BAGHBAN

God has his own ways. Though he took away my dear wife and left me bereft, he blessed my children to excel. Both of us had lived for them, and they had fulfilled all our dreams. Our four children made us proud parents. I would say that is our greatest treasure and our greatest wealth. I consider all my daughters, sons-in-law and their brilliant children to be precious diamonds, pearls and jewels.

Life is very different without Krishna. But, as they say, the show must go on. It was tough to help my daughters settle and it took me great time and effort. Only by God's grace did I find the finest matches for them. My family and I were lucky that Sanjay too found himself, his soulmate in Kamakshi. Great.

That completes the family.

My Diamonds: Sujata and Her Family

On 22 March 1991, my first child, Dr Sujata Singh PhD. was married to Dr Ranbir Singh PhD, an alumni of IIT Madras and settled in the USA.

Ranbir is a brilliant scholar who has a patent against his name in the USA. He comes from an illustrious family. His father, the late Major (Dr) Y.S. Verma retired as a professor at PGI Chandigarh. Ranbir's elder brother, Dr Jagmohan Singh Verma is the Head of Cardiology at Fortis Hospital, Mohali. Dr Jagmohan is married to Dr Yash Bala, a top gynaecologist in Chandigarh, who is more like a daughter to me. They are blessed with a wonderful girl Dipu (Deepali), who is another budding doctor in her own right.

Ranbir and Sujata are blessed with a daughter and a son. Sejal, my first grandchild, studied at Columbia University and is a very vocal activist, forceful orator and a very bright and intelligent girl. She recently graduated from Harvard Law School, having been awarded the David A. Grossman Exemplary Clinical Student Award. Now she is a practicing lawyer. Their son, Rohan, is a tall and dashing young man who has recently graduated with honours from the University of California at Berkeley. He now works with a PE company in San Francisco itself.

True diamonds with an everlasting shine!

My Pearls: Sarita And Her Family

I was lucky to find a good match for my second daughter Dr Sarita (Avantika) Nath (D.D.S.). She married Dr Rajneesh Nath, an M.D., on 15 April 1992. Dr Rajneesh Nath is an excellent diagnostician, who studied his MBBS at Maulana Azad Medical College, New Delhi, moving to the Manipal Institute to do his MD and his super-specialization in Oncology in Vienna, Austria.

Rajneesh has an illustrious family background. His father, Prem Nath, retired as Executive Director of the Airport Authority of India. His mother, Smt. Raj P. Nath, graduated from Miranda College, and was a substantial woman. Rajneesh's sister, Seema, is a Management graduate and is married to an engineer, Rajinder Mendiratta. They are blessed with two sons: Rahul, a bright young engineer and Raghav, an exemplary and brilliant advocate in the making.

At the time of their wedding, Rajneesh was working as a senior oncologist with Batra Hospital. He was in the process of starting his own practice, with a dental clinic for Sarita. But again, destiny had something else in store. Rajneesh received a call from doctors at the University of California who were impressed with a paper he had written and offered him a job at UCMS, agreeing to make arrangements for his new family. He first started as a research scholar there, resigned and joined Johnson & Johnson, USA as a Senior Director. Now, he has his own consultancy which is doing extremely well.

Sarita and Rajneesh are blessed with three brilliant children: Ruhi, Riya, and Ravina. Ruhi has worked as a Clinical Research Coordinator at Stanford University. She has graduated as MPH (Master in Public Health) from Harvard University. Riya has joined Dentistry in Tufts University School of Dental Medicine, Boston and the star of the family, Ravina, is an all-rounder in Class 8. Ravina is particularly dear to me because she chose to change her name, adding my wife's name to her own as a middle name, she is now Ravina Krishna Nath. God bless them all! Ruhi, Riya and Ravina are the true pearls who will radiate purity wherever they go.

My Jewels: Savita and her Family

My youngest daughter, Dr Savita Singh (MD) was married on 7 November 1996 to a bright young man, Niraj Singh, an engineer from Pune and an MBA from the University of Scranton, USA specializing in Finance. Savita, or Baby as I call her, is an ophthalmologist. After her MS (Opth.), she proceeded with a Cornea Fellowship at L.V. Prasad Eye Institute, Hyderabad.

However, she could not pursue ophthalmology in the USA and opted for Rheumatology. She now runs a remarkably successful independent clinic. Niraj must be mentioned for supporting her in her remarkable career. Niraj himself is a very successful professional. He has been a **Top of the Table** member of the prestigious body MDRT continuously for the last 15 years. He was inducted into the Hall of Fame of John Hancock Financial Services in 2016. Niraj was also my source of inspiration. He encouraged me to start a financial services business after my retirement.

Niraj comes from a bright family. His father, J. R. Singh retired as a senior commander from Indian Airlines and his mother Dr Usha Singh was the respected principal of a school. Niraj's sister, Deepa Kapoor and her husband Rajeev Kapoor, are successful doctors in their respective fields. Rajeev is the Medical Superintendent of MMM Hospital, New Delhi. They are blessed with a brilliant daughter, Muskan, a budding architect, and Umang, a brilliant young boy who shows much promise.

Niraj-Savita are blessed with two wonderful sons, Manav and Varun. Manav is an introvert but sharp and, at such a young age, has been bestowed with the Citizen of Philadelphia award. He is a very sober, intelligent boy full of determination and willpower, soon heading to Yale University. Varun is a gem of a boy, sharp and a very lovable child. I must say that all my grandchildren are awfully close to me and Varun has a special place in my heart. God bless him.

Both the jewels are adorable, focused and destined to go places.

I had desired for at least one of my daughters to remain in India. But destiny has its own design, and everybody reached the USA. In a way, it is better that all the sisters are near each other instead.

My Baghban: My Son Sanjay and His Family

When Sanjay came into this world, he brought great joy, especially for his mother and for me too. He completed the family. When he spoke his first word, when he walked his first steps, when I used to give him an oil bath, like my father did for me—every milestone he achieved made me admire him more.

What an amazing and independent person he has become now! He has his own personality, his own thoughts and opinions, and his own sense of humour. I celebrate his individuality and uniqueness and am proud that he is part of my life.

With his strength and resilience, he has seen me through my happiness and my disappointments with equal tenacity. He is incredibly precious to me and as a father, I feel there are very few like him. But even as a contented man, he is still ambitious.

Sanjay started working while he was still in college, interested right from the beginning in finance. He chose the stock market as his route to fulfilling his dreams. At the age of eighteen, he visited the stock market rink and conducted business with hand signals; now, he uses technology.

It's only through his business acumen, perseverance and passion for technology that, within a short time, we went from being a sub broker to becoming a full-fledged member of all the stock exchanges in India. Our venture is now affiliated with foreign exchanges too. But the stock market being what it is, one must look at the graph both ways. I am happy to see that Sanjay learnt his lessons the hard way and grew stronger; he is doing extremely well now. Apart from our thriving business, he is very well-respected in his industry. He was President of the CPAI (Commodity Participants Association of India). This post is generally held for a year, but in his case, the body overwhelmingly decided that he should continue for another year. He completed the second year in January 2019.

I am lucky that when it came to Sanjay I did not have to look for a worthy daughter-in-law by myself. He found his soul mate in Kamakshi, and fell head over heels in love with her, deciding to spend the rest of his life with her.

Sanjay got married on 14 December 1999, on my birthday, to Kamakshi. She studied in St. Stephen's and is a law graduate. She is intelligent and full of warmth, and belongs to a family of standing. Kamakshi's father, H.V. Goswami retired as the Chief Secretary of Government of Manipur and Renu Goswami, her mother, is an excellent person. Kamakshi's sister, Ketaki Goswami Luthra is an intelligent, well-connected and well-qualified advocate married to Siddharth Luthra, ex-Additional Solicitor General of India; he is brilliant at his work and has earned a great reputation. His very name arouses a sense of respect among his fraternity. Ketaki and Siddharth are blessed with two gems, Samarth and Soham, both intelligent grown-up boys ready to take on the world. God bless them all.

I would like to recount an instance which demonstrates Sanjay's loving and caring nature. One evening, much before his marriage, he was setting off for Chennai to meet a close friend. I had gone to see him off at the railway station. He got into the compartment and was sitting at his seat by the window. I stood outside the compartment on the platform, waiting for the train to start and to wish him a good journey. We were talking casually but I could see that something was disturbing him. Very hesitantly, he told me, 'Bauji, I don't want to go to Chennai right now. Kamakshi had a fall and I want to be with her today and tomorrow. I will go to Chennai the day after.' I immediately assured him and asked him to alight from the train. As soon as he got off, the train started and left the station. We did not even cancel the ticket. I could see the happiness on his face—a treasure to me.

Kamakshi is a very loving, caring and respectful woman. One does not come across daughters-in-law who are so caring, she looks after me like a mother especially when I am not well. Her sense of decor and greenery makes the house look aesthetically beautiful.

Kamakshi and Sanjay are blessed with a wonderful daughter, Tejaswi, and a son, Dhruv. Tejaswi is a brilliant star who has, even at such a young age, numerous academic credentials to her credit. She is a good swimmer and can swim up to a hundred laps at one go. She is also a voracious reader like her parents and has ambitions to work in publishing. I feel she is well on her way to fulfilling her dream. By her efforts and with God's grace she has joined Oxford University last year, opting to study English Literature in keeping with her love for language.

Dhruv is a brilliant young boy with an innovative mind, especially in the field of computers and he once assembled a CPU on his own. He is undertaking classes for Python programming. He is still young but I am sure he will go places. A well-balanced, respectful boy who is extremely thoughtful and caring; a bright and shining star.

Both my Tejaswi and Dhruv, the true Baghbans of Rawal Clan. May God bless them with good health, prosperity and happiness always.

13

REWIRING NOT RETIRING

Work after Retirement

By December 1999 all my children were married, and I was alone in Delhi. Lil Bahadur was by my side. As I was still on the job and was terribly busy by myself, the vacuum did not strike me till I retired on 30 September 2000.

Before my retirement, I was selected as the CEO of another multinational corporation based out of Japan in the same industry. The day after my retirement I went to join them and informed all my children of this decision but everyone vetoed it. Enough was enough, they said. I had worked hard and I had to relax. I was inclined to agree with them because I found the culture and ambience of the new corporation to be different from what I was comfortable with. So I rang them up to tell them of my decision not to join.

By 2000, Sanjay had established himself as one of the most sought-after stock traders in Kolkata and was doing extremely well. But since I lived by myself, he decided to shift to Delhi. We would together start as a sub-broker. Accordingly, I found an office space to rent out located in the basement near our house in C. R. Park, and that is where we started our office in 2001. With God's grace, we moved to our own office in Nehru Place in 2008 and became a Member of NSE, followed by other Exchanges. We have one office at Gurugram and Chandigarh. Apart from that, we have business set-up in Singapore and have tie-ups with other major stock exchanges abroad!

To be relevant, I appeared for a few financial exams, cleared them and became qualified to start my own wealth management business, covering insurance, mutual funds, government bonds, RBI Bonds, post office and so on. Again, by God's grace, right from the day one—rather, even before that—I started getting business from my acquaintances and friends, attesting to the fact that my relationships were strong and that my friends trusted me.

The very first year, I qualified for the 'Member Million Dollar Round Table', which is a rare distinction for a man of sixty-two, and in the very first year of entering the industry. I was honoured by the world body at the conference in Las Vegas in June 2003. I continued to retain the membership, year after year for six consecutive years. LIC was so happy with my work that they published a calendar with my photo. It was a great honour. I was selected as the preferred distributor for Mutual Funds. In the year 2008, I was also nominated as the Best Financial Planner in the country.

I would attribute my successful work after retirement to what Sanjay is doing, and doing so well! My work gelled with his line of business, though it is only a miniscule part of his reach. When people ask me what I am doing, I tell them that I have my own company run by my son, and I am the boss.

Most people are not as lucky to have specific responsibilities after their retirement, which affects their life and health. I now have a business of my own and Sanjay to take care of my well-being.

Retirement and the ageing process have their own perils. On one of my favourite morning walks, in the year 2007, a heavy fly hit my left eye which initially I thought would subside with a cold-water splash but the pain increased by evening and I had to rush to the eye hospital. May because of that or other reasons, I was diagnosed with Macular Degeneration in my left eye resulting in loss of straight eyesight from this eye though I was given around 15 injections in my left eye and laser treatment too but it did not improve. Down the line I developed glaucoma as well. With God's grace both aspects have been taken care of with regular medication.

Life after Retirement

One always finds it difficult to engage in activities after retirement. I feel I am blessed. I was President of the Amrit Spastic Society, Noida, and in 1993, I had joined the Air Force Golf Club, and I enjoy golfing immensely now. I was elected President of ATS Village RWA in 2014-15, selected as the President of Gracious Living Foundation (GLF) 2018-2020.

As Chairman of the Open Group, there is always something or the other to which I can contribute—whether in terms of administration or HRA. My own separate Financial

Investment Advisory, as a separate entity, gives me space to work independently within the overall ambit of Open Futures.

Social networking is in my genes right from the beginning. I have been sort of an extrovert since my childhood. I had a good group of friends who formed a musical group named 'Club25' which was founded by Shyam Gopal, who has been my close friend for the last 60 years. It was a wonderful group, and everyone enjoyed the evenings once in a month where we would invite different artists to perform. Every evening was fun. I was President of 'Club25' for three years. As we realized the exclusivity was being compromised, down the line, we a small group broke from Club 25 to form our own group G4; this lasted almost fifteen years. Unfortunately, it broke up recently. We had a wonderful time together, taking trips within the country and abroad.

I was asked to join another group called 'Tarannum', a forty-year-old musical society. They nominated me as a committee member. Though there is a committee, it's president, Gulshan Rai Khurana—respected, versatile, well versed with Urdu poetry— who keeps it alive. Tarannum has possibly the exclusive distinction of hosting the best of the artists of the country at different times.

Another musical group I have joined is Oldie Goldie, a wonderful group full of life with live wire members in their sixties, and together we sing and dance. It's the brainchild of Vipin Agarwal and his wife Meena Agarwal. They are the lifeline of the group. Vipin ji who owns Woodsvilla Resort in

Ranikhet arranges a trip there, every year; taking the whole troupe there is such fun. Pleasure to be a part of this group.

DELHI GYMKHANA CLUB

After retirement, the biggest change in my lifestyle must be credited to becoming a member of the Delhi Gymkhana Club (DGC) in December 2009. Since then, DGC has become a sort of second home to me. I find DGC to be one of the most prestigious clubs of the country, and most of its members are of high standing—half of the total membership are from the armed forces and bureaucracy. It is an excellent place to visit and interact with like-minded people. One can indulge in games, intellectual interactions and a variety of dining and drinking options. In addition, there are regular book clubs and plenty of other entertainment available there.

This 105-year-old club still possesses an old-world charm. As per convention, the elderly are given extra care and service. I visit the DGC almost every day as I am fond of playing rummy. As a routine I reach my office around 11 a.m. and leave for DGC around 4 p.m., and after a game have a drink and return home around 9 p.m. for family dinner time.

To add colours to my being a member, for three consecutive years, I was on the Governing Committee, from 2014-2017 and I enjoyed every bit of it. Apart from being a member of different committees, I was the Chairman of the Entertainment Committee (twice) and once a Chairman of the Administrative Committee. Luckily, the members appreciated my work and I was again on the board for the year 2019-20.

Krishna Foundation: Dedicated to my Wife

Over the last few years, I have been strengthening my dream and desire to start a foundation with the sole objective of helping meritorious students who come from families below the poverty line. I would prefer to primarily aid girl students—but not necessarily.

I am naming the Foundation in my wife's name as she was the fountainhead for inspiring-encouraging and motivating our children to excel in their studies. May be the fact that she was not much educated herself- she had resolved to make Education as her Priority. I wish to take forward her wishes extending a helping hand for underprivileged children.

Foundation will help students in acquiring the skills to practice a trade, to conduct further studies, or even to prepare for competitive exams in fields of engineering, medicine, or civil services. It would help them pursue a course of their choice, not limited to these fields, if they possess the zeal but lack the financial support, the foundation will play its part in such a scenario.

I envisage that this foundation will be different from other similar financial aid programs. I want to offer more than just my money. I would like the foundation to involve with their families, and collaboratively consider how the family and community can be uplifted. I would also want to monitor the student's progress every six months and motivate them throughout.

Once I have aided more than a dozen children and families, I would like to host a yearly event celebrating their successes.

To build and start a foundation requires time, financial

commitment, and management; I have already taken a few, baby steps, in terms of sponsoring:

i) I have already sponsored two students (will start after they pass their 10+2 examinations with a minimum 90 per cent marks in May-June, 21) from Gyan Shakti Vidyalaya, Noida (an after-school program for children from the Jhuggi Jhopri of the Yamuna bed) to complete their higher education. One girl expressed her desire to become a teacher—I have committed full support for her studies up to B.Ed. (may be M.Ed)

ii) I have also announced to facilitate higher education of two students from a computer coaching center, which is run by a friend, Commander Ajit Wasu, for the children of the servants-maids and workers at Sainik Farms.

iii) I have sponsored two students from a poor family, paying their tuition fees, to enable them to study at the Indian Institute of Mass Communications.

I hope to expand this philanthropic mission and consider this to be my 'life goal'. If, and when, I succeed in my endeavor, I will feel happy and contended that I have, in my own little way, contributed back to the society that has given me so much.

AFTERWORD

Satpal Rawal was born to a rich landowner in the Okara district of what is now Pakistan with the proverbial silver spoon in his mouth. He had all the facilities, a constant entourage and privileges only accorded to wealthy zamindars or landowners in the British colonial era. However, after Partition, he quickly found himself virtually destitute, selling homemade sweets and cigarettes at a Railway station platform at the age of seven to help his family make a living. He then worked his way up, steadily over the next seven decades, to where he is today: a Chairman of one of the top three trading and wealth management firms in India.

He was the first in his family to graduate from college, and always prioritized education. His children today are entrepreneurs, engineers and doctors, and his grandchildren are educated at Columbia University, the University of California at Berkeley, the University of Washington at Seattle, Harvard, Tufts and now Oxford!

Rarely has one man journeyed so far, seen and endured so much, and eventually, overcome almost impossible odds over the course of eighty years with sheer determination, grit, positive attitude, willpower and some good luck. This is his story.

Dr Rajneesh P. Nath, MD

ACKNOWLEDGEMENTS

A few people have changed the entire pattern of my life and I would like to thank all those friends who showed me the way forward, who helped me at different stages, who remain connected with me since long, who are sincerely attached to me and their friendship and support gives me the satisfaction of a life lived well.

The first among them was Mr Swami. Had he not referred me to Gestetner, my life would have been altogether different: I might have gone into the family business, or remained with LIC. I don't know if it would have been better or worse, but surely nothing would have matched the kind of lifestyle, joy, achievements and prestige I got from working for Gestetner. While it is true that I had to work hard and every step was a challenge to prove myself worthy of it, yet I accept and am ever thankful to Mr Swami.

In Chennai, Krishna and I were lucky to meet Panna Lalji Tatia and his family. Panna Lalji is an extraordinary and inspirational man and his wife, Chanda is my beloved sister. And dear to me is their son, Bharat, his wife Sangeeta and their daughters, Shobha and Chandana. I miss their eldest daughter, Vandana, who was a gem. I am happy that their son-in-law, Antriksh is so close to my Sanjay and Kamakshi.

Two other gentlemen I would like to thank from Chennai are the late K. B. Lall and his wife, whom we called Jiji. They were my rummy mates. I also extend my gratitude to the late P.N. Dhawan who was the General Secretary of Punjab Association and extremely helpful.

The late Kahan Chand's family must be mentioned. He was my cousin brother and a dear friend. His family and I remain in constant touch—Gulshan, Babli, Sonali, Manali, Raunaq, Ria, and Gur Sahej. God bless them all.

It is a pleasure to mention Poonam Dutt and her family. I appreciate and value her exemplary spirit. She has two wonderful sons; the elder, Gaurav married the beautiful Sonali, and they have two adorable children Anaira and Garv. The younger, Saurabh, settled in London and is married to the lovely Reena Jobenputra and they are blessed with Prince Vir. Poonam is a very sincere and honest person and her heartfelt note for me forms an integral part of this book

While I was posted in Bombay, in 1972-74, I met the Bharuchas, which was a blessing. Through them I got to know, with pride, others from within the Parsi community i.e., the Tatas, Maneckshaws, Bhabhas, Palkhiwalas and others. Shernaz and Rustom Bharucha, are blessed with Jehanara and Danesh. Jehanara is more like a daughter to me. She is a brilliant architect, married to Jehangir Poonawala, and have a daughter, Princess Iyanah—a lovely bright girl.

I spent thirty-six years in Gestetner and I made several friends there. At the top of the list was the late D.D. Mehta.

We were so close that we completed each other's sentences and were often known as *'Ram aur Shyam jodi'*. I am still in touch with Pushpa Mehta—Bharjai ji, and her sons Ranjit, Sonu and Bobby.

Others from Gestetner with whom I am still in touch are Tanvir Bahl, Paramjit Singh 'Romi', Hemant Sharma, Sushil Pasricha, Bhupesh Sharda, Jessie Joseph, Harjit, Neil Todd, Ashok Sharma, Tapan Chatterjee, Pawan Seth, Umesh Kukreti, Satish Sidana, Shashi Lall, Naresh Khurana, Pradeep Kumra, Capt. S.K. Malik, Ashwani Chopra, G.S. Sabharwal, Prakash Oja, Shashi Koley, Deepa Menon and M.L. Pasricha. Unfortunately, three friends have passed away recently due to Covid-19—D.N. Rajguru, A.S. Wadhwa and Sujoy Roy—I will miss all of them. Sujoy, in fact, helped me edit this book in the initial stages. Thank you, Sujoy. May the Almighty give his wife Sudipta, who is like a sister to me, the strength to cope with this loss. And I will miss Rajguru, as earlier and invariably he would drop in during the Durga Puja festivities to exchange greetings.

My friends, those who have kept in touch over all these years are dear to me. Leading the pack is Shyam Gopal—a very lively person and his wife, the late Neena Gopal—who was more like my sister. We always looked forward to Rakhi and Bhai Duj. They have three sons, Ashish Gopal, Anurag Gopal and Anish Gopal. Ashish is an ENT doctor and ever helpful.

Ramesh Sachhar, an amazingly simple God-fearing person, who lives a contented life in this fast world. We joined LIC almost at the same time in 1959, and have remained friends ever since. I hope the best for his children Chimpu and Divya who stay in Dubai.

As I have written, Delhi Gymkhana Club is like a second home for me. My friends there run into hundreds and it is difficult to mention all the names. It is a pleasure to be at the Gymkhana whenever I get a chance, especially to be with my rummy mates. Heading the pack is my dear friend Wing Commander, Duj Nath, and all other die-hard rummy players.

I will fail as a friend if I don't mention my ever-helpful and dear B.S. Brar, a gem of a person, along with his wife Jeeti Brar, son Sangram "Leo" Brar and daughter Masha Brar.

Of course, the pleasure, pride and satisfaction one derives, comes from the family first but it is also a hard fact, especially after retirement, without friends—life remains as if half-lived. As such I am grateful to the Almighty who bestowed upon me a wonderful family and great friends who have contributed in their own way to what I am today.

MESSAGES

S.N. Shrivastava, IPS
Commissioner, Delhi Police

I was left wondering when Rawal proposed that I write a few paragraphs for his upcoming autobiography. It dawned on me that a person who has had such a long and amazing experience must pen down his thoughts for the next generation of readers. He has gone through such unique experiences that it is interesting to read and understand him better.

It did not take me long to see the warmth and depth in Rawal's personality. He seemed to be a sincere and pleasing man, and our infrequent meetings attained regularity. Though our vocations were quite different, we developed a healthy respect for each other. He has endured separation from his native land, and has had to build a life from scratch. It indeed has been a tumultuous journey, involving health issues and the loss of his wife. But the difficult past has only strengthened his resolve and never has it dented his zest for life.

I attended family get-togethers on his invitation to celebrate so many milestones. His daughters, all settled abroad, had come along with their families. I saw that Rawal truly is a 'family man'. In the absence of his wife, he took on the role perfectly. His son adores his father and they are jointly in business now, and the transformation that this has effected is commendable. He has kept himself relevant while moving into different fields.

The colourful shirt that he wears on occasion is not the only reason for his colourful and amazing personality. He refuses to accept that age should make one take life easy: he plays golf, goes on vacations, and enjoys social get-togethers. Very few will match his immaculate sense of style. He is an excellent singer and occupies center stage on cultural evenings, and even plays the synthesizer to complement his artistic abilities. He lives life fully and it is difficult not to be affected by his presence.

For the past few years he actively participated in the activities at the Delhi Gymkhana and was elected as Gymkhana Council member, in-charge of cultural activities of the club. He remained a popular member of the Council and was instrumental in initiating several cultural activities, which are still being vigorously pursued.

~

Vishwavir Saran Das
Former Executive Director, Reserve Bank of India

I am incredibly happy to learn that my dear friend, S.P. Rawal, one like my elder brother, is writing an autobiography and I feel privileged that he considers me worthy of mention in it.

Rawal and I have known each other closely for the last forty-four years; meeting each other when we were both posted in Nagpur (Maharashtra) and shared the same accommodation as paying guests. I remember him as a very handsome, immaculately dressed, suave, **dashing, generous and fun-loving personality. He has hardly changed** over the years and retains his charming aura. I began my career in RBI at Nagpur in 1976 when Rawal was the Regional Head of the leading multinational company, Gestetner. I was thoroughly impressed by his commitment and drive towards his work and determination to achieve his goals—qualities which I would imbibe going forward in my own professional life. Nagpur, in those days, was a rather dull town, but along with a few other friends, we lit it up and had a gala time together. How can I forget his keen interest in my matrimony, how he strongly recommending me to my prospective father-in-law, Prof. K.D. Bagai for his daughter Nalini's hand? It turned out that Prof. Bagai had been his Guru in college.

After Nagpur, Rawal and I moved on in life, getting posted in different cities. Sometimes we would lose touch with each other, but destiny invariably reconnected us. After all, the foundation of an enduring bond had been laid. Post retirement, I am associated, albeit informally, with his family concern, Open Futures, in an advisory capacity for the last eight years, and I am graciously treated as a part of his family.

I have often heard snippets from Rawal himself about his eventful life. The Partition wreaked havoc on his flourishing family and they had to rebuild. And they did. The lesson that one can learn from his life's storybook is to accept misfortune stoically and be humble and graceful when the going is good. Another valuable lesson is to never give up and to have the tenacity, ability, and grit to rise from the ashes like a phoenix.

Rawal has been a pillar of strength and support for his family. He has been a great friend to many and is extremely popular in any social gathering—he stands out! He has not given up on acquiring knowledge and new skills and remains active in running his family business with his capable and talented son, Sanjay. He is an active member and office bearer of the prestigious Delhi Gymkhana Club, plays golf and is a keen connoisseur of music, besides being a singer himself.

May God always shower His divine grace on Rawal and his near and dear ones and grant him a long, healthy and peaceful life.

~

B. L. Vohra IPS (R)
Former Director General of Police, Tripura

Sometimes in life you come across wonderful people who become your close friend right from the first meeting because of their magnetic personality. S. P. Rawal is one such person. I met him about a decade ago when he came for an interview to be a part of the prestigious Gymkhana club of Delhi; I was part of the Managing Committee at that time. He was recommended to me by a very close family friend. Needless to say, we all unanimously voted in his favour. He has now become a darling of the club. The more I see of him, the more I'm convinced that a person not only inherits their great qualities but acquires many others due to their determination, perseverance and hard work.

The story of his riches-to-rags-to-riches life bears ample testimony to his determination and attitude. His life story is worth reading and emulating.

I wish him and his autobiography a great success.

~

Shamsher Singh

You have designed and constructed your own life, brick by brick. I would say your life has been like 'poetry in motion' and it is a story of true human efforts and human glory and, finally, it is a triumph of the human spirit.

**From my youngest brother,
Shamsher 'Khalsa' and his wife Kiran**

~

S.R. Wadhwa
Former Chairman, Income Tax Settlement Commission

Victory of will power!

I have had the privilege of knowing Shri S.P. Rawal for over two decades.

He was born into a well-to-do family of landowners in undivided Punjab (now in Pakistan). Shri Rawal faced unprecedented deprivation early in life, At the tender age of seven, he had to walk many miles with a caravan to reach the Indian side of Punjab. Having left everything in Pakistan, he started his career by selling homemade sweets on a railway platform.

But his determination to excel led him to acquire higher education, even while earning a living during by doing sundry clerical jobs.

The wheels of good luck moved slowly, but surely. From a clerical job, he was selected for a technical post in the famous UK-based company, Gestetner. There, by sheer dint of hard work, sincerity, and honesty, he rose to be its Vice-President and retired after working for thirty-six years.

But life for Shri Rawal was not a bed of roses even after this. He lost his beloved wife when he was only fifty and was left with many responsibilities. But he rose to the occasion, displaying rare courage and fortitude. Now, with his son, he runs a company providing total financial solutions, a company among the top ten companies in share arbitrage and mutual fund bonds insurance business in India.

Shri Rawal enjoys the company of his grandchildren. He is a keen golfer and has found a large circle of friends; he often regales them during social functions with his melodious songs.

I am sure his autobiography will be a source of great inspiration to his readers.

~

Cmde JS Shergill, NM
Former Executive Director, **National Maritime Foundation**

GENEROSITY, THY NAME IS RAWAL!

I have had the proud privilege of knowing S.P. Rawal for almost two decades, having broken the ice on a golf course in New Delhi in 2001. Needless to say, 'Relationships made on the golf course are made for good'.

He impressed with his heart of gold and zest for life. I vividly remember a time, when on the occasion of my birthday, almost soured since I had been denied entry in the Gymkhana Club; my membership cards had not been renewed due to an oversight. Suddenly, this large-hearted gentleman who was leaving the premises, enquired about the reason behind our sullen faces! When he came to know about our predicament, without battling an eyelid he hosted me and my family for a sumptuous dinner as *his* guests. This gesture of his in today's materialistic world has remained etched in our memories and will continue to remain in our minds forever.

His zest for life remains intact despite his advancing years: whether it is playing golf in the dreaded heat of Delhi, socialising, sporting the best of attires, singing, dancing, appearing for examinations, visiting places, throwing parties, acting as master of ceremonies, serving on various committees, he keeps up with it all.

My earnest appeal to him to take it easy have fallen on the deaf years of this restless gentleman. He refuses to let the anchor go or even slow his ship down. Old habits die hard after all!

Being a naval officer, I am reminded of a saying: 'Ships are safe at harbour, but that is not what ships are meant for!'

In tune with this saying, Rawal's risk-taking ability has made him what he is today. He is a role model for any youngster to emulate—that's how I will describe him in a nutshell.

To conclude, a naval salute to you, Sir, from this young man, as he fondly addresses me.

As they say in naval parlance, here's Deep, Mannat and your Young man wishing you fair winds and following seas for the years ahead!

~

Poonam Dutt

Expression of love, affection and gratitude

If I were to scour every word for love and respect in every language, all of them together would not describe my respect for Rawal ji. This is a man who is my confidante, my companion, my best friend. I have often imagined what my life would be without Rawal ji; frankly, it would be a life with a vacuum that could never be filled. This is an individual with fans and friends across the globe, people I have seen drop anything to spend a few hours sipping tea with this man.

Rawal ji has many wonderful attributes but if I were to list them all here then this letter would be longer than the book! So let me pick out two of the most inspiring. My most favourite is Rawal ji's humility. To see a man rise from rags to riches and yet remain so grounded and humble is inspiring. Rawal ji talks to his peers, seniors, friends, employees, clients, children, and grandchildren with the same respect regardless.

My other favourite aspect is his sense of spirit. Rawal ji has the heart of a teenager. I am yet to meet a man with such a fresh outlook on life. While the rest of the world worries about social parameters and proprieties, this wonderful man will look at all situations with such a youthful light and talk purely from his heart, saying what he believes and feels, rather than what he thinks should be heard. This just makes people warm up to him even more. It is wonderfully genuine.

Am I exaggerating, you might wonder. Quite the contrary. I have barely touched on the phenomenon that is S.P. Rawal. He has made my life and me complete. I can assure you once you have read his book you will feel the same love towards this man that has kept me smiling all these years.

I'm truly blessed to be associated with him.

May God bless him with the best of everything, and may he have a long, happy and healthy life.

~

शारदा अरोरा

ये तो वक्त की मुट्ठी में है किस किसको शोहरत देगा हमारे आस पास समाज में इसी सदी के नायक हमारे जीजाजी श्री एस.पी.रावल, जिनके लिए मैंने ये कविता या कहिये गीत रचा, भाव जैसे ही संवेदनाएँ बनते हैं, उन्हें कविता में ढलते देर नहीं लगती।

उनकी उपलब्धियों के साथ-साथ 31 साल पहले उन्हें छोड़कर इस दुनिया को अलविदा कह गईं मेरी दीदी का जिक्र इस गीत में कैसे न करूँ? उनके अपने व्यक्तित्व और बच्चों की तरक्की की तह में उस त्याग मई स्नेह मई मूर्ति का कितना बड़ा योगदान है, ये बिना कहे भी सब जानते हैं।

आया है महफ़िल में कोई, बनके सदी की पहचान
और आया है बनकर के इस महफ़िल की शान

कोई कहे वो साथी मेरा, कोई कहे वो मेरी शान
अपना अपना रिश्ता ढूँढें, ऐसी है पहचान

होते हैं इम्तिहाँ इंसाँ केही, छोड़ जाएँ जब साथ भी
मिसाल बनी है हिम्मत ही, ले आई जो इस साहिल तक आन

आया है महफ़िल में कोई, बनके सदी की पहचान
और आया है बन करके, इस महफ़िल की शान

**A poem by Sharda Arora,
my wife's younger sister.**

~

PART-II
DOWN MEMORY LANE: A VISUAL JOURNEY

THE FAMILY

Happiness galore: With Krishna at Kaithal at the wedding of my youngest brother, Shamsher. Photograph by Jaswant Goomher

Dancing with three of my other brothers at the wedding of Shamsher

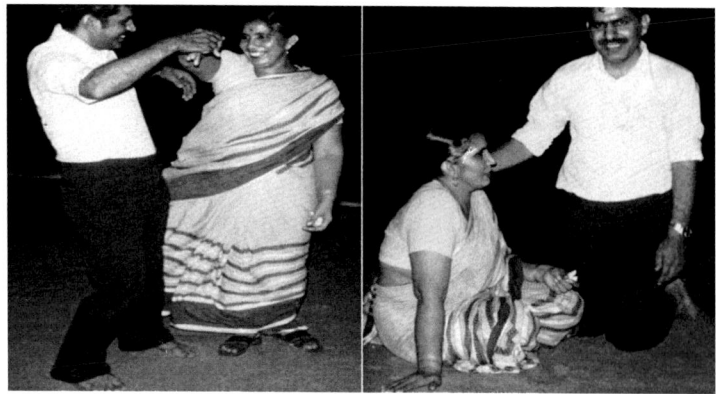

With Krishna at VGP Beach, Chennai

Innocence galore–Carefree: R to L: Baby (Savita Singh), Bunty (Rakesh Rawal), Sarita (Avantika Nath), Sujata (Sujata Singh), Pinki (Yash Rawal, Renu Renu Kohli), Lat (Anil Rawal) and Pepi (Sneh Nagpal)

Jing Bang–the Rawals: L to R: Pinki (Yash Rawal), Lat (Anil Rawal), Baby-Mota (Savita Singh), Renu Renu Kohli), Savita (Avantika Nath), Bunty (Rakesh Rawal), Kitty (Sunita Thakral), Sanjay on Kitty's lap, Bubli (Neelam Ahuja), Sujata (Sujata Singh), Pepi (Sneh Nagpal)

My parents with my son Sanjay

My diamonds

Ranbir Singh, Sejal, Sujata Singh, and Rohan

My pearls

Riya, Ruhi, Avantika Nath, Rajneesh Nath and Ravina

My jewels

Varun, Niraj Singh, Manav, and Savita Singh

My baghbans

Sanjay, Tejaswi, Dhruv, and Kamakshi

Sanjay with Dhruv and Tej

Kamakshi with Dhruv and Tej

Ruhi, my granddaughter, helping me—her Bauji

Growing dream: Tejaswi

The family at my 65th birthday at Jaipur in 2005

With my four children—Sanjay, Savita, Sarita and Sujata

Celebrating my 70th birthday in 2010 surrounded by my grandchildren at The Ashok hotel, New Delhi

Celebrating my 75th birthday on a Mediterranean Cruise in Italy

Four Generations: In my office on my 75th birthday in December 2015

Father: Shri Piara Lal Ji Rawal left for his heavenly abode – 04.12.1976
Mother: Smt Ram Piari Rawal left for her heavenly abode – 27.06.1985

Late Smt Laj Wanti Goomber

Married to: Late Shri Piara Lal Goomber

Late Shri Dayal Chand Rawal
09.06.1932 - 6.09.1982
Wife Late Smt Kaushalya Rani Rawal

Shri Roshan Lal Rawal
DOB: 11.12.1934
Wife Smt Pushpa Rani Rawal
Married On: 30.08.1954

Smt Kailash Rani
DOB: 10.09.1937
Husband Late Shri Kusturi Pahuja
Married On: 14.0[?]

Daughter: Sudesh
DOB: 6.10.1945
Married to: Mr Prabh Dayal Pahwa

Son: Yash Pal Rawal
DOB: 03.08.1958
Married to: Mrs Jyoti Rawal
On 14.02.1982

Son: Anil Kumar Rawal (Lat)
DOB: 18.04.1956
Married to: Mrs Rita Rawal
On: 10.03.1980

Daughter: Veena Ch[?]
DOB: 15.03.1960
Married to: Mr Anil Ch[?]

Son: Jaswant K Goomber
DOB: 23.08.1943
Married to: Late Smt Sushma Goomber

Daughter: Neelam Ahuja
DOB: 31.01.1960
Married to: Mr Omji Ahuja
On 01.02.1979

Daughter: Sunita Thakral
DOB: 26.10.1959
Married to: Mr Praveen Thakral
On: 12.10.1980

Daughter: Asha Chaw[?]
DOB: 12.07.1962
Married to: Mr Hari K[?] Chawla

Son: Ramesh Kumar Goomber
DOB: 20.10.1946
Married to: Mrs Raj Rani Goomber

Daughter: Sneh Nagpal
DOB: 18.10.1961
Married to: Mr Anil Kumar Nagpal
On 20.02.1981

Daughter: Renu Kohli
DOB: 28.12.1960
Married to: Mr Umesh Kohli
On 08.09.1984

Son: Balraj Pahuja
DOB: 28.10.1963
Married to: Mrs Seem[?] Pahuja

Son: Bhushan Kumar Goomber
DOB: 12.08.1955
Married to: Mrs Neeta Goomber

Son: Mr Rakesh Rawal
DOB: 09.12.1964
Married to: Mrs Poonam Rawal
On 01.05.1987

Daughter: Gulshan Chahabra
DOB: 04.09.1964
Married to: Mr Shyam Sunder Chhabra

Son: Parveen Kumar Goomber
DOB: 2.10.1958
Married to: Mrs Sushma Goomber

Daughter: Mrs Seema Chopra
DOB: 25.12.68
Married to: Late Mr Kailash Chopra On 01.04.1991

Daughter Alka Khera
DOB: 19.12.1967
Married to: Mr Ajay K[?]

Father: Shri Piara Lal Ji Rawal left for his heavenly abode–04.12.1976
Mother: Smt Ram Piari Rawal left for her heavenly abode–27.06.1985

 Shri Sat Pal Rawal
DOB: 14.12.1940
Married to: Late Smt Krishna Rawal
15.06.1945-17.02.1990

 Smt. Suraksha Guglani
DOB: 09.02.1942
Married to:
 Shri Hashmat Rai Guglani on: 5.5.1961

 Late Shri Iqbal Nath Rawal
15.3.1944–4.7.1978
Married to: Smt Raj Rani Rawal
On 28.06.1967

 **Mr Shamsher Singh Rawal**
DOB: 09.04.1948
Married to: Late Smt Kiran Rawal
2.10.1950-9.03.2015

Daughter
Dr Sujata Singh
DOB: 07.07.1963
Married to: Dr Ranbir Singh (DOB: 28.06.1958)
On: 22.04.1991

Daughter
Dr Poonam Makhija
DOB: 12.12.1964
Married to: Late Dr Tilak Raj Makhija
On 23.01.1988

Daughter
Ritu Rani Arora
DOB: 25.04.1968
Married to: Mr Vijay Kr. Arora
On 21.09.1985

Daughter
Sherry Grover
DOB: 16.01.1975
Married to:
Mr Dinesh Grover
On 18.09.1996

Daughter
Dr Avantika Nath
DOB: 29.03.1965
Married to: Dr Rajneesh P. Nath (DOB: 31.08.1962)
On: 15.04.1992

Daughter
Dr Shammi Chug
DOB: 30.11.1966
Married to:
Dr Jitendra Chug
On 06.06.1991

Daughter
Jyoti Rawal Sodhi
DOB: 07.09.1971
Married to: Mr Arvinder Singh Sodhi
On 11.05.1998

Daughter
Soneeka Jain
DOB: 18.11.1979
Married to:
Mr Tushar Jain
On: 25.01.2003

Daughter
Dr Savita Singh
DOB: 20.09.1966
Married to: Er. Neeraj Singh (DOB: 27.01.1964)
On: 07.11.1996

Son Sanjay Guglani
DOB: 18.05.1968
Married to: Mrs Deepika Guglani
On 24.03.1996

Daughter
Ekta Nijhawan
DOB: 17.01.1977
Married to:
Late Rohit Nijhawan

Son Sanjay Rawal
DOB: 19.10.1970
Married to: Mrs Kamakshi Rawal (DOB: 06.12.1968)
on 14.12.1999

FRIENDS AND CO-TRAVELLERS

With Lord Meghnad Desai and his wife Kishwar Desai

G 4 Group: L-R: Dolly Bhatia, Sneh Batra, Shuchismita Kapur, Poonam, myself, Narain Kapur, Rajiv Batra & Subhash Bhatia

With Arun Shourie *With internationally acclaimed Indian flautist, Pandit Hariprasad Chaurasia*

With Kathak maestro and Padma Vibhushan awardee Pandit Birju Maharaj

With Kathak dancer and Padma Bhushan awardee Shovana Narayan

With His Holiness the Dalai Lama

With Sadhguru

With former Finance Minister Arun Jaitley, Gen. I.J Singh and Gen. Anil Bhalla

The Arts and Cultural Heritage Trust

Partition Museum,
Town Hall, Amritsar

*About the World's first **PartitionMuseum***

The Partition of India was one of the most defining events in our subcontinent's history. Estimates suggest that up to 18 million people lost their homes and up to 2 million people lost their lives. Yet, almost 70 years after the event, there existed no museum or memorial anywhere in the world to remember all those millions. To preserve this globally significant history, the Partition Museum opened its doors in Amritsar in October 2016 with a curtain raiser. In August 2017, the museum inaugurated all its galleries.

The Partition Museum is a *People's Museum* that aims to tell the stories of the millions affected. It uses their oral histories, personal artifacts, letters, photographs and documents to tell their histories. The galleries showcase objects that refugees carried with them when they travelled; each of these objects poignantly conveys the experiences of individuals and families. The Museum aims to become the largest archive on the Partition, preserving these personal artifacts as well as films, art, literature, photographs and official documents.

The Partition Museum has been housed at the historic Town Hall building in Amritsar, a short walk from the Golden Temple and Jallianwala Bagh. The Museum covers 17,000 square feet, across 15 rooms on two floors. With its beautifully arched verandahs, doors with Venetian glass, heritage floor tiles, and historic belfry (the bell was cast in 1897), the Town Hall is an apt home for the Partition Museum. In the three years since its opening, the Partition Museum has received an overwhelming response from national and international visitors and is on the list of must-see places in India.

The Arts and Cultural Heritage Trust, E1 Green Park Extension, Second Floor, New Delhi-110016
Email:info@partitionmuseum.org; +91-8130001947; Website: www.partitionmuseum.org.

PRINT AND IMPRINTS

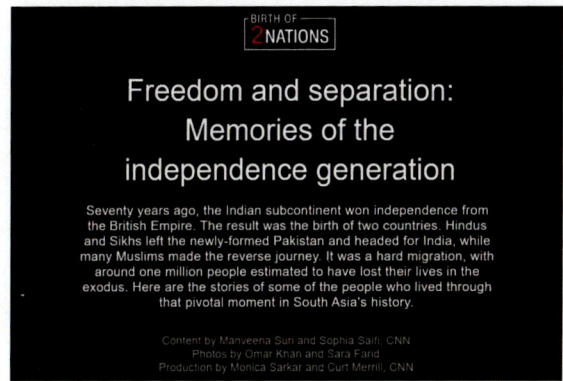

My story was featured in a series of stories by CNN on the lives of people impacted by the Partition (https://edition.cnn.com/interactive/2017/08/world/india-pakistan-at-70/)

*Birth of 2 Nations: Freedom and separation: Memories of the Independence Generation
Seventy years ago, the Indian subcontinent won independence from the British Empire. The result was the birth of two countries. Hindus and Sikhs left the newly-formed Pakistan and headed for India, moment while many Muslims made the reverse journey. It was a hard migration, with around one million people estimated to have lost their lives in the exodus. Here are the stories of some of the people who lived through that pivotal time in South Asia's history.
Content by Manveena Suri and Sophia Saifi, CNN
Photos by Omar Khan and Sara Farid
Production by Monica Sarkar and Curt Merrill, CNN*

■ monthly

Mr Rawal surrounded by his North Zone Branch Managers

North celebrates an outstanding success

Mr S.P. Rawal led his Northern Zone to victory and they celebrated in customary style by achieving 145% of the target for the Battle of Giants. The North sold 33 CopyPrinters during December, creating a new record for the sale of CopyPrinters by any region in one month.

This success has prompted the Northern Region to commit itself to 70% growth in 1996. To quote Mr Rawal: "Success to us is not a destination but a journey."

Mr Rawal's reward for this success is a prestigious Maruti Esteem VX, for which he had to achieve only 120% of his target. Instead of stopping there, he went on to notch up 145%!

Gestetner
Gestetner
Gestetner
Gestetner
Gestetner
Gestetner
Gestetner
Gestetner
Gestetner
Gestetner
Gestetner
Gestetner
Gestetner
Gestetner
Gestetner
Gestetner
Gestetner
Gestetner
Gestetner
Gestetner
Gestetner
Gestetner
Gestetner
Gestetner
Gestetner
Gestetner
Gestetner
Gestetner
Gestetner
Gestetner
Gestetner
Gestetner
Gestetner
Gestetner

April 1989
S. P. Rawal

Thank you very much indeed for all your work and outstanding loyalty to the company over the past twenty-five years.

This is an important milestone for us to have reached together and one which it gives me great pleasure to recognise personally.

Yours sincerely

David Gestetner

Letter dated 24.8.1970 from my eldest brother in poetic form expressing and reporting the state of affairs in the house. He has explained, beautifully, the good points of all the male members co-relating their qualities with their names.

This is perhaps the most unique letter (dated 12.1.1957) ever written by anybody to me, was the one I received from my elder brother Roshan Lal, written on behalf of his son Anil Kumar Rawal, my nephew and the first grandchild of the Rawal family. Every word is depicted with a sign making it so interesting, absorbing and emotionally crafted.

Dated 8.9.70
DELHI-6

आदरणीय प्यारे सतपाल जी,
सदा खुश रहो।
मेरी आँखों के तारे दिल के दुलारे।
हर दम याद आने वाले।
कभी न भूलने वाले।
प्यारे-प्यारे सतपाल जी।

मैं तो पहले ही सोच रही थी कि सतपाल जी को पत्र लिखूँ। मगर क्या करूँ हिन्दी जानती ही नहीं इसलिए पत्र नहीं लिख रही थी। हालाँकि बड़े भाई आपको चिट्ठी दे गये हैं और उसी रोज़ मैंने लाली से पत्र लिखवाया।

अब मेरी गज़ी थी कि बड़े भाई साहब रोज़ खाना इधर से ही खाते हैं। बड़े प्यार से आते जाते हैं। हम भी हर इतवार को पूनम बाग़ जाते हैं।

Letter dated 8.9.1970 by Pushpa Roshan Lal Rawal, my elder Bhabhi (sister-in-law), reflects how close the relationship used to be between a brother-in-law and sister-in-law.

15.11.1970

Respected Brother,
  Sadar Pranam.
  Recd. your kind letter & thousand thanks for the same.
  You are a Great Man, Sir. Your very name that starts with S, & that stands for Successful, & that stands for Senior to all, that stands for Sales & Salesman; but, to me that stands for Super Man.
  At times, I wonder, how miserable conditions & even the worst situations — which otherwise drags even a Gentleman even to the burst-off-fire — fail to affect you. Not a trace even! Isn't it Great. To me, it is an act of a Super Man only. I wish, I could follow you.
  My eye-trouble is gone with the wind. And I am going to Muzaffar Nagar within a day or two only.
  Everything is alright here.
  ~~Sanjeev~~ salutes you, sir.

  With all the Best Wishes,
    Yours Ever
    Iqbal Jah

Pl. reply at 3½, Gandhi Colony, M. Ngr. (U.P.)

Letter dated 15.11.1970 by dear Iqbal, my younger brother, expressing his sentiments and gratitude.

My respected father was in the habit of drafting each piece of writing 'in rough' and rewriting a 'fair' copy. I have picked up this habit from him.

Very interesting graphic impression of Baby (Savita Singh) expressing herself in front of the telephone receiver by folding hands, saying 'Namastey' to me in Calcutta (narrated in Chapter 10)

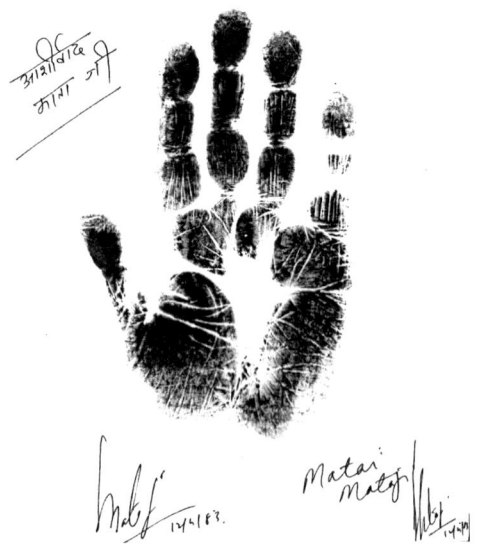

Palm impression of my respected mother dated 12.4.1983

POEMS WRITTEN BY ME FOR MY CHILDREN AND GRANDCHILDREN AND SOME OF THE POEMS WRITTEN BY THEM

Rajneesh's 29th birthday in Janakpuri, New Delhi (just before marriage)

Savita's 26th birthday at Hauz Khas, New Delhi

Sanjay's 21st birthday at Hauz Khas, New Delhi

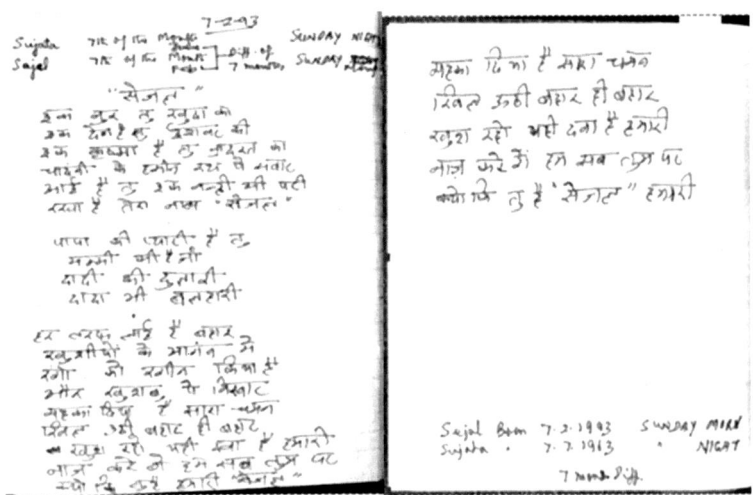

Poem on the birth of my first grandchild, Sejal, on 7.02.1993 at Allentown, Pennsylvania, USA

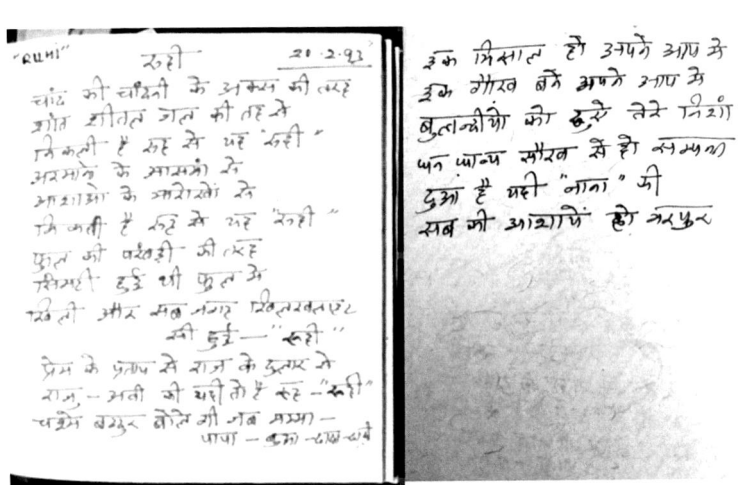

On Ruhi's birth at Janakpuri, New Delhi

Sanjay's 29th birthday in December 1999 at C.R. Park, New Delhi
(just before marriage)

On Tejaswi's birth

Tejaswi's first birthday at Eros Intercontinental, New Delhi

20/7/2003
5AM
P.A. (USA)

Baby का Baby

दो हज़ार पांच सौ दिन और इतना
ही इंतज़ार
मौसम बदले — बहार — सावन — पतझड़ —
शीत और फिर बहार
आते गये — जाते गये और अब आया "मानव"
"मानव" जो मानवता का प्रतीक बने —
मीठा बन के बहार
फूल इस चमन का — महका दिया सारा चमन
बहार ही बहार
ममता के आँचल में सँभाले रखा था
मेरे सीप में मोती — हमारी Baby
हर धड़कन के साथ धड़का है यह 2
— हमारा Sunny

और पल 2 जीयी है — हर सांस के साथ
— हमारी Baby
बरसाती के हर लोग में फुटपाथ है हर
तहर के साथ — हमारा Sunny

और दोनों ने मिल के ख़्वाबो से
पिरोया है इक ख़्वाब
.... मन से "मानव" के लिये
कैसा है यह ख़्वाब
सुन्दर हो — कर्मयोगी हो — सद्भावना हो
संस्कारपूर्ण हो — तेजस्वी हो
और पढ़ो हे मत जी कामना व आर्शीवाद
रख रहा रहे "MANAV" ख्वाबों दे
नाम हमारे — गौरव मे

First child born to Baby after 2500 days of marriage

Manav's birth at Wilkes-Barre, Pennsylvania, USA

मुद्दतों पहले एक ख़्वाब का देखा था
उस ख़्वाब के झरोखों से देखे
उन सितारों के साथ देखा था
यह भी सोचा था कि इस चाँद की इन
और इन दिन इन के भी हो गे
ख़्वाबो में हर जा कोनसी रोशन है
पाईले आई-चाँदनी झिलमिलाती हुई
तेज "तेजस्वी" बन कर
और पीछे — पीछे आया यह चाँद
सच तो यही है कि लड़की ज़्यादा →
पर फिर भी ना सोने क्यों
दिल के एक कोने में इक हसरत →
बागाँ की तरह
और रोशनी ही चलती रहे मेरा

हमने
के तीन झिलमिलाते सितारे
"555" "मेरे
एक चाँद   "झिलमिलाते
चाँदनी हो गी उस दिन   3 भी
झिलमिलाते सितारे   इन के
इसा घर हे जिंदगी मे friends
                     (MINES)

कायम रहती है आई है और रहती रहेगी
भी रहती है

जागेगी →

Sanjay's Son
Born 1·2·2005
AT: 12.12.12
NOON
Read on 19·3·2005
at Banyan Tree
A.F.G.C.

Recited at Banyan Tree, Air Force Golf Club, New Delhi.
Celebrating Dhruv's 1st month in this world

26/6/15 "SPLENDER OF THE SEA"
Day 7 at Sea
- Greece — Italy

The family that we seem to be tied to forever is a distinctly motley crew. But it is from this medley of doctors, lawyers, engineers and predominantly — psychopaths that we seek comfort and a safe heaven. Our unique patchwork of hotheads and lazy-bones works owing solely to the level-headedness & sophistication of one person — Bauji. His aura captures attention and demands respect. Bauji forms the nucleus of the complicated web of our family. He is the gravity that holds us together and fills us with vivacity. Bauji is the reason, after a year of confusion, chaos, sweat and toil from Ani bhah and continuously changing plans that we are all togethered here today. Cheers to Bauji.

.... our super glue
TEJASWI RAWAL

Tejaswi's speech during a Mediterranean cruise in Italy

Dear Bauji,
On your 75th birthday, I want to thank you from the bottom of my heart for being there for us whenever we need you. You are the most enthusiastic, happy grandfather anyone could ever hope to have, and our family is blessed to see your smiling face everyday.

At 75, you can party harder than 20 year-olds. Never change, always be singing, dancing and partying. Stay forever happy and young in spirit!

Love,
TEJASWI
14/12/15

Tejaswi's letter on my 75th birthday

6/21/15

Happy Father's Day Bauji

Happy Father's Day Bauji
You give me warmth by the touch
I'd make you an emoji
because I love you so so much.

I love it when you visit
Same for when I go there
When there's a disagreement
you'll always make it fair.

You are the greatest grandpa
The best that one could have
You had four children
and one became a dad.

Happy Father's Day Bauji
You give me warmth by the touch
I'd make you an emoji
because I love you so so much.

Varun